A WHITE HAT
& ROSE COLORED GLASSES

Unlocking Your Power through Clarity & Action

A White Hat and Rose Colored Glasses: Unlocking Your Power Through Clarity and Action

Copyright © 2016 by Susan Sherbert

All rights reserved. No portion of this publication may be reproduced, stored in a retrieval system, or transmitted by any means—electronic, mechanical, photocopying, recording, or any other—except for brief quotations in printed reviews, without the prior written permission of the publisher.

The concepts in this book do not guarantee success. Positive life changes depend upon the effort of the reader in applying them.

Editors: Christian Pacheco, Earl Tillinghast
Cover Design: Jason Kauffmann / Firelight Interactive / firelightinteractive.com

Indigo River Publishing
3 West Garden Street Ste. 352
Pensacola, FL 32502
www.indigoriverpublishing.com

Ordering Information:
Quantity sales: Special discounts are available on quantity purchases by corporations, associations, and others. For details, contact the publisher at the address above.
Orders by U.S. trade bookstores and wholesalers: Please contact the publisher at the address above.

Printed in the United States of America

Library of Congress Control Number: 2015959770
ISBN: 978-0-9962330-6-4

First Edition

With Indigo River Publishing, you can always expect great books, strong voices, and meaningful messages.
Most importantly, you'll always find … words worth reading.

Praise for "A White Hat & Rose Colored Glasses"

"Susan Sherbert's remarkable insights will help transform your old way of thinking and have you looking at problems from a different angle. Being fearless enough to think big and remove the cloud of doubt and self-defeating thinking to achieve a clear vision are essential for success in the business world. Susan's book gives you all the tools you need to see where you're going and what you need to do to win. A must-read for any entrepreneur!"

> — Mike Ludlum
> Vice President of Operations
> Entrepreneur Magazine

"In Sales camp I encourage my clients to take the next big step in their business. The strategies in "A White Hat & Rose Colored Glasses" are another great tool I can recommend to my clients and business owners to help them face their fears, gain mental clarity, and take more inspired action. When it comes to changing your mindset to be more effective and efficient, Susan Sherbert's book gives you plenty to think about."

> — Ursula Mentjes, M.S.
> President of Sales Coach Now
> #1 Bestselling Author of Selling with Intention and Selling with Synchronicity

A WHITE HAT
& ROSE COLORED GLASSES

Unlocking Your Power through Clarity & Action

Susan Sherbert

Contents

Introduction   ix

PART ONE
What's Wrong with Rose Colored Glasses?

Chapter 1: YOUR VISION   3
    See the things you need to see

Chapter 2: WHERE TO START   15
    Begin with the end in mind

PART TWO
Fear, Obstacles, and Limiting Beliefs

Chapter 3: WHAT ARE YOU AFRAID OF?   29
    Do the things that scare you

Chapter 4: OBSTACLES ARE PART OF LIFE   35
    See setbacks as obstacles instead of problems

Chapter 5: RESISTANCE TO CHANGE   47
    Change is simply doing something different

Chapter 6: IS THE RISK WORTH IT?   57
    The choices we have to make

Chapter 7: FEAR OF JUDGMENT   71
    The emotions and feelings that hold us back

PART THREE
Taking Action and Wearing the White Hat

Chapter 8: TRUTH	87
Be honest, especially with yourself	
Chapter 9: ACTION	107
The actions you take determine everything	
Chapter 10: PRIORITIES	121
Do the right things	
Chapter 11: COURAGE	139
Stand up for your beliefs	
Chapter 12: GRATITUDE	157
Appreciate everything	
Chapter 13: DETERMINATION	167
Never give up	
Chapter 14: CONCLUSION	171
Acknowledgements	177

Introduction

In my first book *Grown-ups Don't Skip*, I focused on showing grown-ups how to have more fun and enjoy life by learning to think like an excited little four year old. I am very proud of the ideas within those pages and I believe in that message one hundred percent, yet this next book is so much more! It takes that "think like a child" foundation and blasts the concept into a whole new dimension. What I did not fully realize when I wrote that first book was the massive impact, and pure power, that comes from the mindset of a child.

The exciting news is that we were all kids once! That means our confident, fearless, and open-minded attitudes are still within us somewhere. Imagine how many obstacles, fears and limiting beliefs we could overcome if we could tap back into the magic power of the simplified childlike thinking we once had! Dreams would be easier to find. Failures would seem like mistakes or "boo boos" instead of feelings of defeat or rejection, and of course there would be tons of creativity and imagination. Best of all we would see a world full of possibility instead of hopeless negativity!

I whole heartedly embrace the potential of childlike thinking, yet at times I may get overexcited and let too much fun slip into my writing style. I realize that is not always popular in the competitive business environment, but I just cannot help myself. Fun and happiness are an important part of life too! I mean really, just because you are an adult who wants to be successful doesn't mean

A White Hat & Rose Colored Glasses

you have to read boring material. It is so frustrating to me. Why can't a book be both empowering and enjoyable at the same time?

Hopefully *A White Hat and Rose Colored Glasses* can help you shift some harmful beliefs, fuel your passion and motivate you to take action towards a successful life you will love. I am confident that these pages will be a mind opening experience for you. The problem is, the adult in me also knows that I only have about a page and a half to prove it.

So let me work my magic and begin by wrapping an important lesson around a simple story. As a result I hope to leave you with plenty to think about and maybe even an unforgettable "aha" moment of inspiration. Here we go…

A puffy yellow car

It all starts in an ordinary yard on an ordinary day. A little girl around the age of four is cheerfully scooting around in one of those puffy plastic push cars. You know the ones with the wide yellow pillars supporting a rounded yellow roof. Anyway, as she cruises down her imaginary highway in that plastic little car, she has to suddenly stop to avoid an obstacle in the road. Her mother is in the way like a gigantic tree blocking her path.

Beep Beep! She honks. "Get the #*&$ out of the way!" There was a frantic gasp, followed by total silence as all eyes turned to the sweet little girl behind the toy wheel. You can imagine the shock and horror on her mother's face, especially since there were other mothers and children in the yard. Then quite naturally the child sticks her head out the space that represents a window and holds up her hand.

"It's okay mommy…I'm in the car."

Wow! Can you see the important lesson in that little story? I sure can. Let's ignore the obvious fact that the mother cusses in the car. The thing I want you to see is that somehow, that little girl formed a real and honest belief that says it is okay for people to cuss as long as they are within the confines of a car. She was confident in that belief and responded with full conviction as if it was a known fact! Of course that is *not* the lesson the parents intended to teach their child, but as children we make sense of the world any way we can, and often the lessons we learn are not always accurate. As a result we end up putting two and two together and logically conclude the answer must be six. Then the child's little brain takes that information and files it away as one of the basic rules of life that we carry into adulthood.

What would have happened if that embarrassing little incident never occurred? That little child may possibly have gone through her entire life believing that swearing was perfectly acceptable within the confines of a vehicle. When she gets her driver's license she will be a model driver obeying all the rules of the road. Until someone gets in her way that is. Watch out! Those four letter words will start popping out without even an ounce of guilt or remorse. There will no need to feel bad or apologize to her best friend sitting next to her or to the nervous boy who sits next to her on the way to the prom. In her own mind, the lesson that she learned was that it is perfectly okay to swear in a car.

If you look at your own life, how many beliefs do you have that may not be true? How many lessons did you learn that were not the message that was intended to be taught? Maybe the first girl who broke your heart drove a puffy yellow car so you are now skeptical to date women who drive yellow cars. Maybe you buy into common beliefs that rich people are greedy, sales people are pushy, or that touching a frog will give you warts. Who knows how our immature brain makes those mental connections that we live by as adults. Maybe now is the time to bring some clarity into your life by unlearning your unspoken rules that may not be true after all.

A White Hat & Rose Colored Glasses

The Holiday Ham

Here is another lesson disguised as a story but you may have already heard this one. If so this time I want you to focus on the bigger picture instead of just listening to the words. Again we go back to our little girl from the toy car only this time she is a bit older and a bit wiser. Since there were no hard feelings over the incident in the puffy yellow car, she proudly watches as her mother preheats the oven, takes the ham out of its wrapper, and warms the sticky ham glaze. Next her mom picks up a knife and carefully cuts one end off the ham, swirls it around, and trims the other side. Perplexed our inquisitive little girl asks, "Mommy, why did you cut the ends off the ham?"

"Gee, I'm not really sure, dear. I guess that is how my mother taught me." The child gets off her stool, goes into the other room, and puts her elbows on her grandmother's lap. "Granny? Why did you teach mommy to cut off the ends of the ham?" Again, there was a confused look. The grandmother responded, "Well I suppose that is just how I was taught. Why don't we go call your great granny and see what she has to say?" When great granny gets on the phone, her response is "Darling child, what makes you ask such a silly question? Back in my day the ham was simply too big to fit into my pan."

All right! Another insightful moment! How many things do we do simply because that is the way we have always done them? I have an entire chapter dedicated to the resistance to change because change is scary, uncomfortable, and just doesn't feel right. We prefer to do things we know, understand and are familiar with. That is the easy way to go. Not to mention that tradition is umm, tradition. It's just how things are done - don't mess with it. A thought shift that might be helpful here is to learn to bring back our wonderful childlike thinking ways and start

Susan Sherbert

asking that annoying little question "Why?" Asking why goes a really long way to finding the clarity that will change, well, just about everything.

It was only a lime

Here is one more story and it began when I was in line at the grocery store. The woman in front of me had just done the final tap to pay her bill when her husband came rushing up holding a lime. Apparently they needed a lime for a recipe they were doing that night. The lady, who reminded me of a grown-up version of our puffy car girl, turned to me and politely asked if I would mind if the checker rang up her last minute item. It was only a lime so I gave a *don't worry about it wave*, turned to the checker and said, "It's okay just add it to my order." No big deal right, again it was only a lime?

Well, this is the point where all of that adult thinking comes rushing in. Here stood a fully grown adult woman and she was practically stuttering with unspoken anxiety trying to figure out how to respond. "Er, Oh no! Really you don't have to do that," she said all in a fluster. Gee I had thought I was doing a nice thing, and all she wanted to do is refuse my offer. Why all the stress?

To me it was a bit like looking at a scene with a thought bubble pointing at her head. I imagined it went something like this: *I can't take money from a stranger, in fact I shouldn't even be talking to strangers. If I take the lime will there be strings attached? Will I feel obligated somehow? What does this stranger think of me? I can't impose on her to pay for my stupid mistake.* Wow, there is simply way too much thinking going on here.

Of course she finally accepted my offer to pay for the lime, but before she left the store, I heard her mumble something to her husband about having to "pay it forward." What? It was only a lime! Do adults really think that way?! Of course we do! There is a lot of stuff happening in our head. Now if I had offered to buy a child a popsicle, the kid would most likely have responded "Thanks lady!" And a smile of appreciation would be all that was required. Yet as adults, our subconscious thoughts can run wild and really complicate the simplest of things.

Remember - pure childlike thinking is still within us somewhere. We can learn to question our beliefs, ask a lot of really good questions, and clear out some of the complicated old junk that we carry around with us every day. The secret to success in life, and in business, begins by clarifying our thinking and becoming aware of the unwanted thoughts and feelings that could be blocking our path. It will certainly be a bumpy ride, but the journey back to where we began is a trip well worth taking.

Not what you want to hear

It is time for me to put on *my* good guy hero white hat because I must do what is right, and have a difficult conversation. Unfortunately even with all of the stories and lessons within this book, they won't do you one bit of good unless those life altering awareness moments are followed up with real world physical actions. I am truly sorry to have to break the harsh reality to you but this book cannot fix your problems. That is something you, and you alone must do. I hope the tidbits of information I provided here will assist you in finding your big bold dreams, true vision, or meaningful purpose, but the actions you take, or don't take, are all up to you. I realize it sucks to hear it but there are no quick solutions or short cuts. Only actions. If you are being totally honest with yourself at this very moment, I would hope that you are starting to comprehend that you contribute to both the obstacles and the successes in your life. That is probably something that is uncomfortable to hear, and you may even be feeling a little resistance or fear right now, however like it or not, it is time to accept the fact that you are responsible for the changes you desire.

Please don't let those words stop you! Instead turn the resistance into a challenge. Confidently put on your very own good guy white hat and do the things you know you need to do. That means the first action you must take is to simply get started. That can be a really difficult thing to do, and luckily I address fears, blocks, and other reasons why we stay stuck, later in the book, but don't let your inspiration fade away before you even give your new beliefs a chance to grow! Take that meaningful first step and take action! There is so much strength in getting started, why not do something simple like make a commitment to read this book? That's it. Read a book. You can surely handle that one action.

However, whatever action you chose to start with, turn it into a commitment by keeping an open mind and allowing new and uncomfortable ideas to sink in. Don't give up when you disagree with something you read or hear some negative comment. And don't let your hectic life be an excuse not to try, to stay stuck, or avoid finishing what you started. Face your fears. Keep your promises. Take better actions!

Once you become aware of just how much weight your thoughts and feelings have over the actions you take, you can then begin to shift your mindset and adjust your priorities. Change will happen if you begin replacing old worn-out beliefs that no longer serve you, such as cussing in a car, and replacing them with bigger, stronger and bolder ways of thinking. I hope you allow this book to be a tool to assist you in redefining what is important because if you are not playing the game of life with clarity and action then you are at a disadvantage. Now go put on that wonderful white hat, adjust your rose colored glasses, and let's get started!

A White Hat & Rose Colored Glasses

> WHEN YOUR THOUGHTS, FEELINGS AND ACTIONS WORK TOGETHER YOU TRULY CAN CREATE THE LIFE OF YOUR DREAMS

Why A White Hat and Rose Colored Glasses?

Almost every motivational book, workshop, or program is founded around some combination of three basic concepts: thoughts, feelings, and actions. These three elements have changed countless lives and they are the key to changing your life as well. Focusing on your thoughts and behavior to produce better results is an almost universal message of success…however instead of using those three words to describe this book, I have reduced my motivational vision down to just *two* words: Clarity and Action.

WHITE HAT: Good guys wear white - well at least that is how I see it in my simplified childlike way of thinking. Good guys put on their white hat and do the right thing. They are heroes that are confident, courageous, and never ever give up. They are honest. They are brave. When there is a job to be done or your world needs saving, you want a good guy on your side. One of my favorite sayings is about not confusing kindness with weakness because there is no doubt that strength and integrity are woven into the fibers of that wonderful white hat.

Little kids wear white hats every day yet they are totally ignorant of the power it holds. It is not until we grow-up that we begin to fully understand the struggles, risks and sacrifices that it takes to claim the honor of possessing something as special as a white hat. It is a symbol of all things good so it baffles me as to why anyone would want to wear anything else. We will discuss that point later but the important thing to realize is that in the context of our adult way of thinking, I use the image of a white hat to represent the hero. Not a hero in a book or a movie, and not the real life men and women that do unbelievable things. The hero that I am talking about is you.

I want you to put on that white hat and become the hero in your own life. I want you to do the things you know you should do, and then be proud of your actions. Can you imagine the thought shifts you could have if you begin to remember even a tiny part of that courageous little kid that believed that they could change the world? For the purpose of this book, I have chosen a white hat to represent the actions a hero takes to transform mental thoughts into positive real world results.

White Hat = Action

Changing your thoughts is the first step towards success, but following up those insights and "light bulb" moments with the right action is what will help get you unstuck from whatever is holding you back. Be the hero in your own life and be proud to wear a white hat.

Rose Colored Glasses: As you can probably tell by now, I frequently wear rose colored glasses and I don't see anything wrong with that. Who wouldn't want to see the world through a positive lens? Would the world be a better place if everyone put on dark glasses and focused on the negative energy? Because of my belief in the power of childlike thinking, I like to use rose colored glasses as a symbol for improving our vision. I see them as a tool to help us clarify and focus, not as blinders to reality. Rose colored glasses have gotten a bad rap. Anything that accentuates the positive should be a good thing. Wearing rose colored glasses helps us gain insight into our own thoughts and feelings so we can see the changes that need to be made.

I truly don't understand how wearing rose colored glasses is seen as a bad thing. As kids life was simple and our parents

A White Hat & Rose Colored Glasses

protected us so our vision was pretty good. We didn't need to wear glasses. We just sat back and enjoyed the day. Well, as responsible adults life has changed quite a bit since then. We have no choice but to live in a world of reality. We have commitments, jobs, and family. Fears, worries, pressures, and failures are all too common in the grown-up world. People let you down; but they also lift you up. You laugh, you cry. You feel joy and experience pain. This is all part of the real world we live in. Welcome to life.

Just as a white hat is a symbol of action, I see rose colored glasses as a symbol of clarity. Look at your thoughts, feelings, and limiting beliefs and try to see past those blocks to find your true vision. Learn to know when you are wearing your rose colored glasses and when you are hiding behind your dark glasses. Life is made up of both positive and negative, good and bad, and the right set of specs can help you see the world from a well-rounded perspective. Bad parts of life exist but it is up to you to see beyond them. Learn to focus on the possibilities of a world full of creativity, love, and change for the better. A strong vision has the power to open your mind so that you may begin to clearly focus on the things that truly matter in your life. To me, rose colored glasses don't limit or block vision - they enhance.

Rose Colored Glasses = Clarity

One other point is that glasses are not laser eye surgery. That means we don't wear glasses all the time. We put them on and carelessly take them off. Sometimes our vision is fine. It's on track and we clearly see our life and the direction we are headed. Other times we get so stuck that that our vision becomes out of focus and unclear. We don't even realize we have our dark glasses on. Corrective lenses are helpful because they give us insight into our thoughts and behavior. They allow us see both the positive and the negative so we can embrace what is working and fix what is not.

Susan Sherbert

In my childlike mind I see rose colored glasses more like x-ray vision or night vision goggles. Those devices are used to discover things that are hidden, blocked or hard to find. How cool is that!

To improve your vision close your eyes and focus

Wearing Rose Colored Glasses...

- **Improves creativity and imagination**
  Promotes better problem solving skills that lead to new ideas

- **Builds confidence**
  Brings out the hidden qualities and talents people already possess

- **Means facing obstacles with courage**
  Improves communication, leadership, sales and success

- **Encourages change**
  Reduces fears that lead to stress, complacency and poor health

- **Adds a level of fun**
  More energy and joy lead to better job satisfaction and higher productivity

- **Reduces judgment and negativity**
  A positive outlook encourages more participation

PART ONE

Be Proud To Wear Rose Colored Glasses!

Anything that has the potential to harm us, real or imagined holds the most power in our mind. Positive things are nice but when our brain thinks we are in trouble or in danger, fear wins every time.

Negative images and thoughts are really illusions. They are simply warning signs to beware. They remind us to be cautious and careful. Unfortunately we often over react and end up full of panic and fear.

This is where the rose colored glasses can be really be helpful. If we can train our thoughts to think careful instead of fearful, then the negative parts of life won't hold so much power.

I am not saying that we should put our heads on the sand and become oblivious to bad things. I'm hoping that you can use the rose colored glasses to help you find clarity and understand that the bad stuff isn't really as horrible as it first appears. The purpose of this section is to improve your vision so you can see both the negative and the positive. I believe that once you truly begin to see the positive side, the possibilities, your life will start to change for the better

Chapter 1

Your Vision:

See the things you need to see

Before we get to the actions required to wear a white hat, we must first uncover the power of our rose colored glasses. We need to find clarity. We need to see the things we need to see - and that starts by paying attention to our thoughts and our feelings. Our brain is a good place to begin because its main purpose is to keep us safe. It's like the ultimate protective mother always vigilant and on guard. Our brain is always on the lookout for danger and instinctively focuses on anything, physical and/or emotional, that may cause us harm. How nice is that to have someone looking out for us? The problem is, we are adults now so sometimes all that caution gets in the way. We need to go out, make mistakes, learn, live, and take chances. Yet our over-protective brain is always with us telling us to watch out and be careful.

> IF YOU DO NOT CHANGE DIRECTION, YOU MAY END UP WHERE YOU ARE HEADING
>
> — LAO TZU

A White Hat & Rose Colored Glasses

Changing your life starts by changing your vision

I cannot begin to explain the importance of connecting to the positive thoughts and feelings that will become the vision of your dreams. Unless you are living the life you imagined, or are totally satisfied with where you are right now, then you need to work on improving your vision. They key is to put new images and thoughts into your head. Pictures of something better, something grand, something bigger then you think is possible. Changing your thoughts and allowing those "crazy, I could never do *that*" ideas to hang around for a while is what will help get you unstuck and moving in a better direction. When your total focus is on worry and stress there is absolutely no room for anything else in your brain. I mean really, who has time to think about the future or dream of a trip to Hawaii, when their entire brainpower is being consumed trying to figure out how to afford rent?

Helping people shift their thoughts and find their dreams is one of the biggest reasons why I am passionate about teaching adults the value of childlike thinking. I get excited when a stubborn grown-up finally decides to put on those rose colored glasses and take a peek at the possibilities of things they may have not been ready to see before. I know if they can find just one tiny speck of something different, then there is unlimited potential for their future. But first they have to embrace that unfamiliar spark and allow new thought shifts to happen. This can be difficult because often the critical image we need to see is no bigger than a poppy seed - like a tiny speck in a pile of dirt.

Finding that first seed is vital. All it takes is a tiny blip, one small spark, and an idea is born. That fleeting thought has the power to shape your future and until you find that mind-altering form of energy, you will remain stuck. But before we continue, let me point out that it isn't just one spark or one seed. Your magnificent brain will produce thousands of seeds of inspiration in your lifetime. Some images, in fact many, will take hold and flourish when you are ready. Other nuggets of wonder will never produce a single harvest or even see the light of day. But everything and I do mean everything, starts with a single thought in your head. So let's get going and try to find these tiny suckers!

WAKING UP YOUR IMAGINATION STARTS WITH POSSIBILITY

Where do seeds come from?

Mother Nature has her secrets and where seeds come from is a truly interesting question. Therefore my childlike thinking mind has come up with a creative answer that I can use to make a point. The way I see it, seeds come from within the plant. I don't know how they get there, but a plant knows how to make seeds from the resources it already has. All of the elements exist and when the time is ready, seeds begin to form. It's just like that with your vision. Your inspiration already exists. It is within you right now. We just have to wake it up, take action, and make some space so it has room to grow.

Looking at it that way, the problem isn't really making the seed because we produce seeds all the time and don't even know it. The task is to find the seed so we can plant it in a better location. That can be tricky because in the beginning new ideas are so small they barely exist. As adults our creativity and imagination declines because too often we allow it to become out of shape from lack of use. When this happens our vision becomes limited and out of focus. Plus there are studies that show that our peripheral vision shrinks as we get older. A child tends to see the entire picture whereas grown-ups tend to focus on specific areas. Our vision becomes distorted because our attention becomes limited to the issues that are right in front of us. The result is that we clearly see reality but forget about the power of possibility - which is one of the most powerful tools we possess. The ability to acknowledge that things could be different has the power to create thought seeds that can change a life forever, yet we see problems not solutions. We see pressure and responsibility, instead of unrealistic dreams. And according to the law of attraction, what we focus on, the images that get the most attention, are the harvest that we produce.

> *Your actions are producing seeds and you don't even know it*

There are tons of things getting in the way of us living a better life, and we will discuss many of the obstacles blocking our path later in this book, but let's start by strengthening the biggest, most important, mind muscle we have. It is time to get our imagination back in shape.

Imagination

Imagination is what creates your vision and holds onto the images your mind flashes before you. Trusting in things that you don't yet see as possible requires blind faith. Your imagination is the tool you use to persuade your brain to go against all logic and believe in the fairy tale, the happily ever after, or the billion dollar dream. It has to sell the idea based on a few powerful passionate images that are not backed up with facts and data. Your imagination has to play mind games and win.

Is it any wonder that people have a hard time finding their purpose or motivational vision? If your imagination isn't in shape then finding that perfect vision will be difficult. You must have total confidence in the pictures your imagination draws. Your ultimate dream or make-believe destination must be so strong that you believe down to your toes that this incredible journey will be worth the effort.

Imagination is one of the first things to go as we transition into the grown-up ways of thinking so it is one of the first childlike traits we need to bring back. If you want to move forward, face your fears, or break out of your comfort zone it all begins with your imagination. It begins in your head with your thoughts. Not the same old worn out pictures that your brain recreates over and over every day. You need fresh ideas that are motivating and different.

CHANGE STARTS BY PAYING ATTENTION TO THOSE CREATIVE NEW VISIONS IN YOUR HEAD. IT MEANS PUTTING ON YOUR ROSE COLORED GLASSES AND SEEING THAT THE IMPOSSIBLE IS NOT SO IMPOSSIBLE AFTER ALL.

In order for any type of change to occur you first have to see the finished results, in your head. You have to visualize. You plan your path and mentally envision the outcome you want for your future. Many people use this visualization technique to succeed in the real world. Top athletes, motivational leaders, life coaches, yoga teachers, and just about anyone who wants better results from life use some form of visualization. Imagine that in order to remove your blocks or improve your situation you start with visualization.

Can you see why my excited childlike brain is going crazy right about now? People truly do understand the power of imagination! Whooo Whoo! They get it… but what I don't understand is why adults are so stubborn and set in their mature ways of thinking that they insist on calling this powerful technique *visualization*. Why can't they just call it what it is: *Imagination*. A world of make-believe!

Creating new mental images, painting fantastic scenes of the future, and living in a world where anything is possible is nothing but pure childlike thinking! It's bold, creative, and full of unlimited opportunities and dreams. I call that imagination! And guess what? Imagination was with us long before we could even spell that other sophisticated grown-up word.

> Visualization is just the grown-up word for Imagination

If you have heard of the law of attraction then you know that in order to remove our mental blocks and live the life we desire, we need to visualize our end results and allow the power of imagination to do its thing. This is super-important because that image, those made-up thoughts will motivate our body to take real action and manifest unbelievable results.

Imagination creates negative images as well

Your imagination is so powerful that it also creates all kinds of imaginary problems and conjures up some really frightening bogeymen type of thoughts that are just waiting to get in the way. We will go into conquering our fears later but I just wanted to point out that discovering your ideal vision is where we must start. However simply creating that awesome mental video to play in your head doesn't mean the road will be easy. But that is reality. I guarantee there will be unexpected detours on your journey but a clear strong vision, and childlike confidence, is what will get you back on track and keep you moving forward.

One thing we can do to slow down the negative side of our

run away imagination is to put on our rose colored glasses so that we can begin to see past the obstacles that we think we will encounter along the way. The grown-up mind will fully accept our life changing vision but we must at least acknowledge that yes there is a negative side as well. What we need to do is trick our minds into believing that our new vision is the best thing in the world! That it is so desirable that we can handle anything that comes our way and that the bad stuff isn't really that bad. The images of your ideal future, or the obstacles in your path, are nothing more than a figment of your imagination. Good or bad, it's all just make-believe. So focus on your positive dreams and start making up some really good stuff!

Bringing back dreams and possibilities

To help you envision the importance of finding your vision let me bring back a story from *Grown-ups Don't Skip*. It begins with the wonderful world of possibilities. Try to visualize the following scene: You are in a nice warm bed. You wake up in the morning and decide to go outside for a look around. That means you have to drag yourself out of bed, put on some clothes, and face the outside world. You would rather stay inside and watch television again, but you'll play along with me to keep the peace. You open the door and scan the entire horizon. You see nothing. Every direction is the same. You live in the middle of the flatlands, so it doesn't really matter which direction you travel. Everything looks the same, so your day begins and ends with nothing to motivate or guide you.

Then one day you get up and put on your new rose colored glasses. When you look around this time things seem different somehow. The warmth of the sun is soothing, and you don't remember the last time you heard birds chirping. Your vision is

A White Hat & Rose Colored Glasses

more focused so this time you think you see a mountain far away on the horizon. You can't be sure it is there – it might be just your imagination - yet the possibility of a mountain now exists. If that is true then there might be snow. That means there is a chance that you could build that snowman you have always dreamed of. Heck you might even be able to play in the snow or maybe, just maybe, there is a ski resort on the other side. Imagine that.

What direction do you think you will be heading today, the next day, and the day after that? Towards the mountain of course! The simple possibility that there is something out there on the horizon, beyond the limited adult imagination, is a very powerful force. You now have a direction to move toward, and a dream of things you never imagined possible. Even if the mountain was all in your imagination, it doesn't matter because you had a place to start. You got out of your rut and began to imagine all kinds of new adventures. The moral of the story is that once you see the possibilities, the imagination takes over, dreams begin to form, and the journey of a lifetime begins.

Finding your North Star

We don't have to know all the answers in life and you can never fully predict where your journey will take you. In fact you will never have all the answers or overcome all the obstacles. Yet if you can find your spark of inspiration then getting to your destination will be a whole lot easier. Think of your wants and dreams like a compass or the North Star. As long as you keep an eye on your North Star you know you are moving in the right direction. Your dream isn't real, it is simply the image in your head that motivates you and gives your life purpose and meaning. A clear bold idea in your head is what helps you focus and stay on track. That image keeps you from getting lost. Nothing more.

Susan Sherbert

YOUR ACTIONS ARE WHAT GET YOU WHAT YOU WANT. THE IMAGE OR SPARK IS SIMPLY THE LITTLE LIGHT TO GUIDE YOU ALONG THE WAY.

What do you want out of life? If you don't have a grand vision, a North Star, or don't even know what you are passionate about, you are not alone. I can explain all the secrets in the world about creating that end vision of where you want your life to go but if your imagination is still rusty, or you are not ready to let go of your reality based beliefs, then those creative images will elude you. By now you know that the change begins in your brain. Your purpose is in there somewhere you just have to put on your rose colored glasses and start looking. Start by looking for a flash of possibility, or a spark of imagination. This can be difficult because adults don't easily allow those "useless" or "unproductive" images to stay in their thoughts very long. They squash most of the unrealistic ideas and never give the inspiration a chance to grow.

Maybe I can help find your guiding light if I tell you about how I found my spark of inspiration that turned into one of my big, bold lifetime dreams. Even though my childlike thinking was, and still is, full of creativity and imagination I almost lost my dream because of the influence of my grown-up thinking friends.

I had no clue what I was passionate about, but every book I picked up seemed to talk about the importance of having a lifetime dream. I agreed with them but my brain was still stuck so I temporarily filed the idea away but still gave my brain permission to play with the idea. I was patient. I was aware. I paid special attention to every new and unusual image that popped into my head. I tried not to toss anything out as a crazy idea! I was open and receptive to thoughts that were outside my comfort zone.

Then one day it hit me! Bam! A vision of my future that I really, really liked. I could totally imagine it! I was going to golf every course in California. How many courses I had no idea.

A White Hat & Rose Colored Glasses

How would I get on all of the private courses? Who knows? Who cares! Just imagine all the possibilities! This will be fun! And who knows maybe someday I'll even be able to write a blog about it. So there you have it. One crazy little idea that all began with a tiny spark of imagination!

> ONCE YOU SEE THE POSSIBILITIES, IMAGINATION TAKES OVER, DREAMS BEGIN TO FORM, AND THE JOURNEY OF A LIFETIME BEGINS.

A fairway of dreams

Carrying my fragile little spark of imagination I excitedly went to share my vision with my reality based, grown-up thinking golf buddies. I was sure they were going to like the idea. How could they not? They are my friends after all. Well this is the place where more often than not, things really go wrong. Totally wrong. How quickly I was brought back to the adult world of reality and limited possibilities. "You can't do that," they all said. "Do you know how many courses there are? And how are you going to get into all of the private clubs?" I thought these people were my friends and would support my dreams, not squash them down to nothing.

Reality based adults just can't help themselves. They are only trying to help and they feel it is almost their duty to inform others of all the hardships that will happen along the way. It is their way of protecting you, keeping you safe from heartbreak and disappointment.

> MOST OF US SHOOT DOWN NEW THOUGHTS ALL THE TIME WITHOUT EVER REALIZING JUST HOW DELICATE THOSE FIRST SEEDS OF IMAGINATION ARE.

Susan Sherbert

If you want your dreams to survive it is up to you to ignite that spark, to protect your vision, and encourage your seed of inspiration to form. You must take caution with those infant thoughts and give the idea time to blossom and grow. If you don't fight to keep your dreams alive then they could easily be tossed aside, left to wither away or smolder down to nothing.

Well I decided to stand my ground and keep that flame burning! I can't let other people decide the direction of my life. It's my imagination, and my vision so la, la, la, I'm not listening! I have learned that when adults tell me all of the reasons something can't be done, I use my imagination and all of the childlike thinking I possess and respond with a reason why it can be done. "You don't have the money to do that," they say. Okay, so maybe I will win the lottery, get a job at a country club or become friends with a golf pro. When you have dreams and childhood imagination, anything is possible.

The funny thing is, as soon as my "adult" friends realized that I was going to live my dream without them, and that my vision may actually be possible, suddenly they became believers in my dream too. "I wonder who I know that could get you onto some of these private courses." They went from skeptic to supporter; reality to dreamer. It takes a bit of convincing before people will join you on your magic journey, but with a little help from friends, all your dreams can come true.

One more point to make; I have repeated that story many times. Once I was talking to a group of golfers so I asked a lady if she had any dreams. She shook her head no. I pushed back and inquired if maybe she would like to play the Pebble Beach golf course. Her immediate response was, "I can't afford it." I then politely pointed out that she just squashed a possible dream without even giving is a micro second to grow. She couldn't afford it - period! End of story. Is it possible that she could have saved up the money to play? Maybe her family could give her a gift for an anniversary, birthday, or retirement. Or maybe a co-worker or vendor has a family member with connections. Who knows? Anything is possible.

Afterwards I happened to sit near her table at lunch and I heard her say, "I did squash my dream, I really did just squash the idea without ever giving it a chance." Imagination, visualization, or dreams; whatever you call it, do everything possible to keep the pictures in your head alive.

Chapter 2
Where To Start?:
Begin with the end in mind

"Are we there yet?" That is a really good question because it clearly shows the difference between how a grown-up thinks and how a child views the world. Kids see the destination and want to know "Are we there yet?" To the grown-up mind this is an annoying question because adults start at the beginning of the journey and know there is a long road ahead. They are focused only on what they can see around them and more than likely they are worrying about something they might have forgotten. The adult mind is drawn to the bumps and obstacles on the road and is on the lookout for any dangers that might be encountered on the way. That is just what the mature brain does. It is doing its job of trying to keep us safe.

The child's mind on the other hand is super excited because a kid clearly sees where they are going. They are so focused on their destination that they can't contain their emotions. They can't wait to get there. Are we there yet? Are we there yet? They don't see the troubles that could happen along the way and they don't worrying about much of anything because the wonderful possibilities that lay ahead are all that matters. They have started their journey by thinking about the end.

A White Hat & Rose Colored Glasses

Start at the end? That doesn't make sense

Starting at the end makes total sense to me but when I mentioned this to a friend, she looked at me like I was a bit odd. Her confusion was probably because I saw something that she just wasn't quite ready to see.

WITHOUT A PAIR OF ROSE COLORED GLASSES ADULTS GET STUCK IN THEIR LIFE LONG BELIEF THAT YOU ALWAYS START AT THE BEGINNING.

A beginning, a middle, and an end - that is how life works. No further discussion required.

Too many adults live their lives with limiting beliefs, and they are unwilling or unable to see a different side or opposite point of view. They dismiss the possibility that their life could be different because they don't look beyond their restricted view of the way things are right now. We are taught certain rules and lessons that become the foundation of our beliefs, and shifting old ways of thinking is a very difficult thing to do. Of course I am not saying one belief is better or that a certain way of thinking is wrong. The inspirational moment I am trying to convey is simply that we need to be more open to new ideas. Be willing to question your old beliefs and be honest if they are not working for you.

If you were asked to re-write the story of your life, where would your journey end? What would you want to accomplish? I cannot tell you how many adults have trouble answering this basic question. A rather common response is, "I have absolutely no idea. I don't even know where to begin."

I know where to begin. In fact I feel like that energetic little kid holding up their hand in class. Pick me! Pick me! I know the answer, please pick me. You begin the journey at the end. You need to create a vision about the outcome you want to achieve. It's the law of attraction. What you think about determines the results you get. Communicating that simple idea can be tricky when people are stuck within the constraints of the grown-up view of life. Hopefully you will "pick me" so that I can help you flip a switch in that grown-up mind and bring clarity where confusion used to exist. So let's get back to the end of this interesting adventure.

Begin at the end

If you don't quite understand this whole start at the end concept yet, don't worry. I have several stories and examples to help your mental shifts start to happen. If you already "get it" please keep reading because it is an interesting journey and you may learn something new along the way.

What happens when you start a really good book that you just can't put down? The reason you are so involved, so drawn into the story, is because all of your energy is concentrated on how the book will end. You have to turn that next page because you can't wait to discover how everything turns out.

Now imagine that you were the author of this book. When you sat down to write that very first page do you think you had the end of the story in mind? Absolutely! Your story has a beginning, a middle, and an end. You begin the book by introducing the characters but a story is usually started with some kind of ending in mind. Of course the end may change and things may not turn out exactly as you had planned, but you started with a plan. Your first step was knowing what the end of the story should look like.

The same idea is true when we decide to take a vacation. In order to plan a trip we have to know where we are going. We can't make plane reservations, plan our route, or get excited about the journey if we don't know where we are headed. The first stage of most travel begins with a destination. Again, like writing the book, sometimes we arrive at a totally different location then we planned, but even before we begin to pack there is some kind of outcome in our head. If you want to reach your destination you have to start with the final results first. You plan from the end first and build the journey back to the beginning.

It reminds me of a conversation from the pages of Lewis Carroll's Alice in Wonderland:
"Would you tell me, please, which way I ought to go from here?"
"That depends a good deal on where you want to get to." "
I don't much care where –"
"Then it doesn't matter which way you go."

Starting at the end is very powerful because if you start where you are now, at the beginning, it totally makes sense that you may find the journey a terrifying path to take. Taking that first step down that long path to destinations unknown is ever so frightening. No wonder your feet are firmly planted on the ground and not moving anywhere. If your vision is only allowing you to see the long road in front of you, the obstacles in your way, then you are not looking far enough ahead. If you can't fully see your dreams, or get excited about the destination, then what is motivating you to get started? Is there any surprise as to why you have not started to move forward yet? If you think you know where to begin but only see what is right in front of you then the entire process is so much harder than it has to be.

I have come to realize that one of the reasons I am continually being told that I don't live in the real world is because I see the world backwards. I begin at the end all the time and never really understood this until one day when I was on the golf course. I commented that it was a really difficult uphill putt. My partner looked at me confused and said, "What are you talking about? It's a downhill putt!" Oh that explains everything! Most adults see their ball traveling from their putter into the hole. I start at the hole and see the balls path rolling back towards my putter. I start with the end and see the world backwards. Wow. That is why I have difficulty understanding why grown-ups do such strange things. It is because I think backwards; I feel that I naturally process the world from a child's perspective by starting with the future, or the end, first.

If I were to continue and try to explain that life should be lived Future - Present - Past then you truly would think I was crazy, so let me conclude this section with these three little tidbits of information:

- **If I was thinking like an adult:**
  I would probably be wearing my dark glasses and my thoughts might be focused on how long this journey is going to take. I would see all of the obstacles in my path and only be focused on the part of the road that I can actually see. Shifting my thoughts and feelings seems like a good idea but all of the childlike thinking sounds like total nonsense to me. It will never work. You don't start at the end. You start at the beginning - everyone knows that.

- **If I was wearing my rose colored glasses:**
  I would be thinking like an excited little child. I would see all of the possibilities that this book has to offer. I would understand that the little insights and inspiring stories might first appear silly but new thoughts take time to develop and sink in. I would keep an open mind because I am starting to realize that the rewards at the end of this journey just may be life changing.

- **If I was wearing my white hat:**
  I would respond, "Quit complaining and keep moving! What's next?"

A White Hat & Rose Colored Glasses

Be you!

Now it is time to shift your limiting beliefs by being true to yourself. Would your life be better if you didn't doubt yourself, question your actions, or ignore your true feelings? To accomplish that you must first reconnect with the thoughts and feelings of that absolutely pure little being you used to be. You have to become aware of who you were as a child. Of course you can't survive in a world with the limited knowledge of a four year old. That would be ridiculous! But that doesn't mean you should forget about the real you, the person you were before you started to accept the ideas, beliefs, and opinions of others.

Who are you? We start as innocent little beings with a blank slate of knowledge, and as our bodies grow our unique personalities start to emerge. We used to always be confident, imaginative, and fearless. At four years old life was hopefully full of fun, laughter and pure joy. We didn't care what other people thought and we had not been stifled by the rules of society, or burdened with guilt, anxiety, or responsibility. Curiosity, passion and courage were in abundant supply. Our young minds were pure and free from status, judgment, discrimination, and worry. All we wanted was a bit of attention and maybe a smile for our efforts. Then we grew up.

ARE YOU AWARE OF THE LITTLE CHILD THAT IS STILL WITHIN YOU? OR HAS THE PERSON YOU USED TO BE BEEN PUSHED ASIDE AND TOTALLY IGNORED?

To help find your inspirations and purpose try to remember what you used to enjoy, or what strong emotions you felt when you were young. What made you happy or sad as a child? What exciting ideas and dreams did your brain used to create? Reality changes our way of thinking but as an adult it is now up to us to choose the thoughts and feelings that we want to hold on to. You get to decide what lessons are still valuable and what beliefs are only getting in your way.

From day one parents try to keep us safe and protect us from the bad stuff. Some of their advice was awesome and their teachings have inspired you to grow into the person you are now. Yet there are other rules that were learned that are no longer beneficial to us in any way whatsoever. For example, if you never talked to strangers, think of all the wonderful people you would never have met or the interesting conversations you may have miss. And I am pretty sure I am old enough to know how to dress so that I don't' catch a cold or get the flu.

It is up to you to become aware of your thoughts and feelings, and begin to sort through your lifetime collection of lessons and beliefs that you carry around every day. Think of it as a time for a closet clean out. Find what fits the person you have become and get rid of what is out of date and no longer serves you. It is time to reconnect with the ideas that inspire you so that you may move forward and let go of the thoughts that could be holding you back. But most importantly you must become aware of who you are and who you want to be.

Look at the list below. Hopefully you will see some of the characteristics and qualities of the person you want to be. And hopefully you will see other traits that you wish to leave behind:

1. Imagination was abundant. Now we live in reality
2. Possibility was endless. Now we focus on the limitations
3. Curiosity was common. Now we are overwhelmed
4. Enjoying the process was fun. Now we want results

A White Hat & Rose Colored Glasses

5. We accepted others as they are. Now we try to change others

6. A carefree attitude easy. Now we must be responsible

7. Life was fearless. Now it has become fearful

All of you

One day I was discussing the idea of connecting with the little children we used to be with two very grown-up thinking sisters. Both were not yet ready to see the potential of childlike thinking but at least the first sister was willing to acknowledge the possibility that an inner child may be lurking around in her somewhere. She jokingly mentioned that people said she grew up with her arm permanently bent because there was always a handbag dangling from it. She loved to play with dolls, dress up, and of course carry a handbag. I was excited to hear that because we were making progress. There was still a bit of her inner child within her because to this day she loves to dress well and carry a matching handbag. And as for the dolls, let's just say that she has a nursery full of them. I am not kidding. She literally has an entire room dedicated to her doll collection.

So here was a person who didn't believe she had any childlike qualities yet there she was a full-grown adult still playing with dolls. Awesome! She was truly connecting with part of the dynamic, nurturing person that she was as a child. Now for the part that needs work. She also lives a life full of anxiety and fears. She will only ride in certain cars with certain people. She avoids planes, bridges, and left hand turns. She refuses to ride in elevators and she isn't comfortable in crowds or even in movie theaters.

This is certainly NOT the strong person she is. She had

experience, an unfair event of the real world years ago when she was in a severe car accident. Bad things happen to good people and those memories and fears have become embedded in her grown-up life. Those behaviors are not who she is and sometimes it can take a lifetime of work to break down the thoughts and feelings that prevent us from reaching the fearless little beings we once were. The reality is most of us will never find all of the child we once were. Nor should we! We are adults now. However too many grown-ups won't let even a part of that wonderfully unrealistic little child back into their mature world of reality. But if you were wearing a white hat, you would see the value of connecting with your inner child and you certainly would never give up trying to bring back those amazing qualities only a child can maintain.

Now on to the other sister - and this one was a tough cookie. She was having none of this childlike thinking stuff and her feet were firmly planted on the ground on that issue. She was not budging one inch; she was a reality-based person and that is who she is going to stay. I had my work cut out if I was going to shift her thinking or even make one small dent in her grown-up beliefs. Then she gave me the perfect opening! During her adults can't think like little kids rant, she boldly defended her position by saying, "When I was a little kid all I did was sleep and eat!"

Bingo! One part of her childhood personality jumped out at me like a bullet. This sister is one of the biggest foodies I have ever met. She loves to cook and she loves to eat. Food is her childhood passion and she didn't even see it at the moment. So I pointed that out and reluctantly she had to agree. Then I pushed it even further. What about that sleeping part? This sister takes her grown-up role so seriously, and that is an admirable quality to have, but she is always tired. This lady is kind, giving, loyal and dedicated to her family. If you need anything, she will be there for you no matter what. Yet sometimes, just sometimes she needs to reach back to that selfish inner child and put herself first. Sleep, who needs sleep? Not the grown-up sister!

If she was thinking like a child she would be sleeping like a baby, but her unwavering belief that other people always come first is firmly embedded in her other grown-up beliefs. She pushes herself even when it is clearly not necessary, because in her way of thinking that is what responsible people do! The whole point is if we could get back in touch with only part of the powerful being we once were, imagine how different our grow-up lives could be. Once we learn to think like a child, and act like an adult, it becomes easier to become the you, you want to be.

A lesson in imagination

Circling back to the beginning of this section I want to remind you of the importance of imagination. It is the mind muscle we must use to find and ignite that spark that will lead to your dreams. With a little practice your imagination will get stronger and exciting new images will be easier to see. As adults we forget about the joy of creating and forget what exciting new thoughts feel like. Imagination is important because not only does it create those flashes of our passion that we use to build new visions but imagination is fun and exciting! It inspires us to want more, to see exciting new things, and to temporarily break free from the stress of our reality based world.

I have a fun exercise that I use to help adults strengthen their imagination. I found this children's game called Ned's Head. It is basically a gigantic child looking head made from fabric with holes in the ears and nose that allows you to reach in and pull things out of Ned's Head. Brilliant! It is a perfect learning lesson for grown-ups. I fill this jumbo head with all kinds of odd stuff and then ask adults to pull something out of Ned's head. Next I ask an

Susan Sherbert

adult to describe what they are holding. Grown-ups usually look at me with a confused look and tell me exactly what the object is. "It's a pot scrubber." This is so totally the wrong kind of thinking! No imagination whatsoever. The object came out of Ned's Head. Ned is four years-old. His head is full of imagination creativity and dreams! A ping-pong ball is not a ping-pong ball to a little kid. With a bit of imagination it becomes a mini snowball with super powers that if used for evil could freeze the entire world. A simple pack of cards could contain secret messages that hold the formula for communication with space aliens.

Are you starting to see the point? Have you allowed your imagination to engage? Grown-ups have to stretch their brains and keep trying, but soon their minds lighten up and come up with fun and creative ideas too. They just need a little push until their imagination wakes up and comes out to play. With a bit of exercise your imagination will come back - just like riding a bike. Once crazy ideas start to pop into your head, pay attention and encourage the foreign thoughts to hang around for a while. One of those strangers could be holding that elusive seed you have been looking for.

Also, you don't have to have the Ned's Head game to practice your imagination. I've done this at restaurants. I'll pick up one of those little sugar packet holders and ask my adult friends at the table to tell me what it is. Again, it takes them a minute to remember where they put their unrealistic thoughts, but soon imagination begins to flow! And who knows, you just may find your dream right there at a restaurant table.*

ONE OF THE MOST POWERFUL TOOLS WE POSSESS IS THE ABILITY TO ACKNOWLEDGE THE POSSIBILITY THAT THINGS COULD BE DIFFERENT

*To see what Ned looks like and to watch my silly video about this lesson visit FunHappyEnjoy.com/how-to-find-your-imagination.

PART TWO

Fears, Obstacles And Limiting Beliefs

Going outside your mental comfort zone is an important part of claiming ownership of your white hat. As adults, fear too often scares us into a rut of comfort, and we end up in a nice safe warm spot and decide to stay for a while.

Giving into fears, especially the small ones, is not a very heroic thing to do. If I could be honest like a four year old I just might say you are acting like a coward.

Fears alert us to potential danger, but try to see the warning signs for what they are - a time to pay attention and be alert! Let fears inspire you to move forward. Don't give in and retreat back into a safe comfortable way of life. Stand up and fight for yourself because that is what heroes do. They face their fears.

Chapter 3
What Are You Afraid Of?
Do The Things That Scare You

Now that we know what we are looking for, that tiny little image smaller than a poppy seed, the next thing we need to do is discover what is getting in our way. What are the thoughts and actions that are blocking your path? There are countless obstacles that could be the cause, and every person is different so that complicates things even further. Therefore finding exactly what is blocking you is a journey you must take alone.

It is time to stand strong and find the courage to face the monsters and demons that scare you the most. This section will help guide you on your quest as you search for the clarity that eludes you. Let's get rid of those blocks once and for all. Enough is enough because if you want peace, happiness, and success, you will have to do the things that scare you.

What are you afraid of?

The world is a scary place and I totally understand why we are afraid of violent situations. Things that physically threaten our lives are dangerous and should be scary, terrifying even. We want that fight or flight switch working correctly so we can get the heck away from danger.

Yet somehow I don't think the fear of pain and injury is our real problem. I'm guessing our biggest fears are mental, not physical. Fear of changes, or being afraid of being judged by others are just the first two fears I thought of that could be holding us back. So let's take a look at some of the other not so violent things that scare us.

A quick search of the Internet tells me what people are most afraid of. A fear of heights, spiders, flying, and germs are on the top ten list, as well as thunder, cancer, and strangers. And here's an interesting observation. Both agoraphobia and claustrophobia are on the list of things that frighten us most. Isn't that interesting? That means we fear wide-open spaces and small enclosed spaces. I'd call that pantophobia – a fear of everything.

And don't forget about the fear of speaking in public! Or here is the last fear on the top ten list: A fear of dead things. Maybe there is more to our fears than I thought. If a fear of dead things is such a strong phobia, then why do we welcome ghosts, skeletons, and tombstones into our lives? Once a year around Halloween we celebrate zombies, vampires, and blood thirsty killers.

Humm, maybe somehow facing our obstacles and demons in a safe atmosphere such as Halloween could help us get rid of the terrifying emotions that get in our way. Maybe we need a month dedicated to flying. Embracing air travel would certainly help to reduce the fear of heights, strangers, and germs. Using the toilets on a plane would help with the claustrophobia, and traveling to any location is a positive step for an agoraphobic.

As for the spiders, well, maybe it's okay to be a bit afraid of a few creepy crawly things. In fact, fear is a good thing and we are supposed to be afraid of certain things. For example, we should all be atomosophobics because a fear of atomic explosions is only natural. On the other hand being an arachibutyrophobic seems a bit odd because why should anyone be afraid of peanut butter sticking to the roof of the mouth? But again, everything always seems to come back to the thoughts in our head, so who knows what people are thinking.

Ghosts, zombies, unknown outcomes and trying new things may all be scary, but they are figments of our imagination. Fears have a purpose but the problem is, sometimes we let our imagination turn our fears into nightmares, and that can be truly terrifying. I don't know, maybe right now I am suffering from samhainophobia – fear of Halloween. But enough of all these crazy fears that other people have. We are here to help you discover the fears that are holding you back. But, here is one last phobia I found interesting. Hippopotomonstrosesquippedaliophobia - the fear of long words.

So many to choose from

Fear is an incredibly destructive force and I cannot even begin to imagine the human potential that has been wasted because people were too frightened to face the imaginary monsters that wreak havoc in our bodies. Some fears are small, such as when someone frightens us with a "Boo!" that makes us jump. Others are so paralyzing that they require professional attention. There are so many different fears to choose from that I could not possibly list all of the things that scare us and prevent us from reaching our potential.

To conquer this vast endeavor, I have broken our fears into four categories. The first are like the "boos" that make us jump but don't cause any real permanent damage. I call these the **OBSTACLES**. They are more like irritating delays that get in the way and set us back. They are more frustrating, than they are scary, but too often they prevent us from perusing our passion so that is why I have included them on the list.

Next comes the FEAR OF CHANGE. I like to think of this one as the silent killer. When something is new or different it often makes us feel uncomfortable. For example let's say we decided to take an exercise class. We have no idea what we are doing so every move seems awkward! We are slow, unsure, and feel really silly. Not to mention we are short of breath, sweaty, and don't smell too good because we are totally out of shape. In other words when we do something unfamiliar we are probably going to suck at it in the beginning because change just feels funny.

Too often we aren't willing to risk looking silly, feeling a bit uncomfortable or accept the failure that is a part of the process. We don't always turn around and run back into our comfort zones, but far too often we talk ourselves out of trying something new because change is uncomfortable! This is where our rose colored glasses are really handy because if we can just keep going we will see that things usually do get easier. With practice the fear of change loses some of its power.

Fear of failure is also a big one. However, to me it's really more about risk instead of failure. So our UNWILLINGNESS TO TAKE RISKS is category number three. It's about the choices we make or more importantly, the choice we choose not to make, that keep us stuck. To face this fear our choices should be made with a focus on success instead of being all about the possibility of failure.

Our last category of fears is so obvious that it could be easily overlooked. It is the FEAR OF JUDGMENT. I think this is one of our greatest fears because it's all about our feelings. Opinions are important; words have power and the people we care about matter. Emotional fears are terrifying because no one wants to feel like a loser, be seen as an idiot, or thought of as insignificant.

To help shift your thoughts and face your fears, I challenge you to find one tiny thing that scares you and make a commitment to do it this week. Make that sales call, ride that elevator, have that conversation, take that class, or even wear something a little different. Start getting used to things that make you feel anxious and do something that is outside your comfort zone.

Fears hold us back because they...

- **Limit the exploration of new thoughts**
- **Prevent people from trying**
- **Don't allow us to ask the difficult questions**
- **Create too many limiting beliefs**
- **Avoid risks and keep us in our comfort zones**
- **Weaken our confidence**
- **Focus on the negative instead of what is truly important**
- **Talk us out of doing the things we need to do**
- **Get in the way of our dreams**

Chapter 4
Obstacles Are Part of Life:
See setbacks as obstacles instead of problems

When you start any new project, adventure, or goal there is a ton of good positive energy. You are excited! Anything is possible! Then right on schedule the obstacles start to arrive. People get frustrated or upset and decide to give up or change directions. Why? It's not like we didn't know problems were coming. Overcoming obstacles is part of life. Challenges are part of the process. The question is do you confront the unforeseen delays head on, or do you turn those learning lessons into gigantic problems? More often than not, the huge monster of a problem is really only an obstacle in your way. It is a blockage on your path not a complex detour or the end of the road. So stop turning unexpected bumps into enormous problems. If you slow down and take a moment to look at the bigger picture, overcoming obstacles will become just another bump in the road.

Become the king of your mountain

If you are motivated and driven to succeed then you have already had to overcome some pretty nasty obstacles. You have

A White Hat & Rose Colored Glasses

climbed mountains you thought would never end, and have battled dragons you never saw coming. Life is both the best thing in the world and the worst. You can make lots of money, but then you have to spend all of your time trying not to give it all back in taxes. Love is wonderful and break-ups just suck. You could totally love your job and wouldn't ever think of leaving. Then a new boss arrives on the scene and you can't get out of there fast enough. Even something a joyous as a new puppy is full of potty training and endless chewing. Life is full of ups and downs. There will always be obstacles to overcome. Get used to it.

If you have a dream and want to live a more successful life, then it is pretty much guaranteed that you will come face to face with some pretty difficult situations. That is just the way it is so accept the hardships and embrace the wins. Sometimes you travel on a road that is heading up the mountain, and other times the road takes a dip heading down. Your path turns to the right and then takes a hairpin turn to the left. It is time to realize that to become king of your mountain, the road is never, ever, going to be a straight and easy path.

I'm too busy dealing with difficult people, meeting impossible deadlines, taking care of family, and having money issues. I do not need another problem in my life. How am I ever going to overcome one more obstacle? But that's what successful people do. They face their challenges and eventually reach the top.

So THE MORAL OF THIS STORY IS IF YOU WANT TO LIVE YOUR DREAM AND ACCOMPLISH GREAT THINGS, YOU HAD BETTER GET YOURSELF A GOOD PAIR OF HIKING SHOES AND START CLIMBING.

Susan Sherbert

We have a problem

I have to confess. I have a few family members who love the word "problem." One in particular is especially fond of it. Every time she gets on the phone she says, "We have a problem." Problem! Alert! Something bad is about to happen. I start to get pulled into her panic and think of all kinds of horrible things. To me problems are like emergencies. They are issues that need my attention now. They mean trouble. Then when I find out that her problem is that they don't have a ride to the airport next week, or that the dog needs to go to the vet, I feel kind of stupid because I got all worked up over nothing.

Because of my childlike thinking I have learned to train my brain to think of day to day problems as obstacles - those I can handle. Most unforeseen situations are more of an inconvenience or detour. They are minor challenges that are just a pain in the butt to deal with. I think this is one of those times when many grown-ups think I live in a fantasy world because I try very hard not to over-react to difficulties many grown-ups see as problems. The reality is that with the help of my rose colored glasses I have honestly learned to see problems as mere obstacles.

Kids are naturally problem solvers and innovators. They don't know it can't be done and aren't even aware there is a problem. Adults not so much - they get too hung up on the *why* and the *how*. *Why are you doing that and how is that going to help? You should be coloring within the lines, and how come that tiger is blue? How are you ever going to be successful if you can't even follow the rules?*

Adult imagination and creativity is limited so their problem solving ability doesn't flow freely. They get hung up on rules and try to color within the lines because that is reliable and comfortable. As we age, new thoughts and images are harder to find and resolving problems requires more and more effort. If you can't see an outcome, or immediately find a solution, the likely conclusion becomes that it can't be done. Without the aid of innovative thoughts minor obstacles quickly become impossible problems.

Creativity fixed my dryer

I suppose I have always been on the creative side, but I never really understood the connection between creativity and problem solving. To me creativity was just the childlike thinking of having fun and coloring outside the lines. It was not until one day someone pointed out that I was unaware of the value of my own creative gift. Humm, value? Creativity is fun, new and exciting. What has that got to do with anything? A lot apparently.

Building your big, bold dream requires forward thinking, and one obstacle that often gets in the way is not understanding how to get there. When some people don't know how to do something, very often they give up instead of trying to figure out a solution. This is where creativity comes in. Creative thinking solves problems and removes obstacles in the way. Open minded thinking helps find new ideas so you can try new things, experiment, and find answers to difficult questions. Creativity requires change, failure, and a passion to learn more.

Okay, that sounds like me. I'm more likely to see a problem as a challenge and I like to figure out ways to make things work. But is that creative? Apparently it is.

One day our dryer stopped working so I was faced with an obstacle. Not a big problem, just an unexpected issue that had to be resolved. We could call out a repair guy but that was expensive, besides, I like to fix things so why not have a look? I can handle this! I got down on my hands and knees and figured out that the burner was not working. Okay, I identified the problem - the flame didn't ignite. But what was the solution? The best place to

Susan Sherbert

look these days is the internet. Wow! Look at that a website full of repair videos. I entered the model number of the dryer and I found the answers I was looking for. Right there next to the video was a place to click and they would send me the part. Brilliant! How easy is that? The part arrived a day or so later and after watching the video a second and third time, I went to work. Of course the screws didn't come off easily, and I had to re-install the part because I put it in backwards the first time, but it's all fine. It's just part of the creative process.

Well look at that! The burner worked! I overcame several obstacles and actually fixed the problem. Doesn't success feel great! Then that darn life thing happed and a few days later, the dryer stopped working again. What, I thought I had done everything right! In fact, I did do something correct because it did work. What went wrong? Time to call a repairman? Not a chance.

I didn't panic for more than a moment and I didn't let one little set back become an overwhelming problem. I tried it and failed. Back to my creativity for another solution. I did not realize that there were other videos for different parts, and apparently some of the parts work together. Okay, so we will be without a dryer for another few days until the new parts come in - not a major problem. Then when the parts arrived, this time I replaced two new parts and what do you know, Plan B worked.

Handling challenges is all part of the process. Success is about playing it smart, avoiding the obstacles when you can and managing the damage when you can't. Whatever challenges you face today, you can be pretty darn sure there will be more challenges to block your path tomorrow. Overcoming obstacles is almost a requirement in life so learn to handle the setbacks without all the drama or panic.

IF PLAN B DOESN'T WORK MOVE ON TO PLAN C

A White Hat & Rose Colored Glasses

A guy who loves grass

To help you see the benefits of improving your creative thinking, I recently asked a friend in a creative hi tech business about his thoughts on creativity and innovation. He responded with a story about a guy who loves grass? What? How dull is that! I can't imagine anything more boring than watching grass grow. He went on to explain that if people love what they do and are passionate about any subject, they are likely to be successful.

This guy who loves grass is super excited about the stuff! He can talk to you for hours on the subject. Again, it all sounds pretty boring to me, but he is fascinated by all of the elements that go into growing and maintaining a lawn. But what does that have to do with creativity? The point is creativity is all about the quest to discover new things. It's about innovation and finding ways to improve the process and make it better. Creative people want to know more and are excited to find different solutions to problems that other people miss. They don't let the how prevent them from trying. It becomes the thrill of the chase for the next big thing.

To help get your dreams moving you need to start with a passion for something and then get excited to learn everything you can on the subject. Start by finding solutions, making mistakes, and creating a different mousetrap. Creative, out-of-the-box thinkers push the limits and build things, or do things that no one has ever thought of before. They are innovators. Pioneers that started out just like the guy who loves grass.

These innovators and trailblazers are also successful because they like obstacles but love problems - the bigger the better. They know there are lessons to be learned and that the new challenges will only make their ideas even better.

Back to this guy who loves grass. He is the perfect example of success and creativity because he is so passionate about these short green blades that he made a career out of it. The guy who loves grass is a greens keeper for a golf course. I didn't see that coming but it makes total sense now. I know very little about growing grass, and my lawn is proof of that. However I am almost in awe of the grounds crew that can keep a golf course looking pristine. As a golfer there is nothing better than a smooth perfectly cut putting green. When the greens are bumpy, patchy, and uneven it is not a good thing. On the flip side when the greens are in good condition the ball moves so darn fast that you would think you were putting on concrete, instead of growing blades of grass. And that is only the putting surface. The fairways take a totally different level of care, and then there is the rough to factor in as well. Add in eighteen holes and that is a heck of a lot of grass to be taking care of.

Even when the guy who loves grass overcomes his obstacles and creates the prefect golf course, he doesn't stand back and admire his work. He takes all of the skills and knowledge he learned and moves to a new location with a different climate, different pests to control, and new grass-related challenges to conquer. His passion and creativity live on because the guy who loves grass enjoys the journey. I often talk about how kids love to build it, smash it, and then start all over again. This goes a long way to solving problems because if you find a passion, enjoy the process of creating, and are not paralyzed by a challenge, then success will certainly be headed your way.

Life plays hide and seek

Even with the best rose colored glasses in the world, you still won't see everything clearly. For some odd reason life likes to play hide and seek with our lessons. We struggle with our problems for unknown reasons and often we don't understand the purpose of our setbacks until much later in life. How many teens think their parents are total idiots only to realize years later that they really did know what they were talking about? How often do we struggle, stress and worry over obstacles that turn out to be the best gift we ever received? We don't see the lessons as we resist, fight, and refuse to accept the things that are there to help us, because at that moment we only see the problems. The lessons come into view later.

Maybe life's lessons are disguised as problems so they can be played out one training exercise at a time. You have to build your dreams piece by piece, frame by frame without ever truly knowing how the entire story will unfold. Life changes, shifts, and takes all kinds of diversions, but it is this mix of experiences that builds the skills you are developing as you slay the dragons and find the courage you never knew you possessed.

It reminds me of this story of a little boy and a butterfly. One day he saw a caterpillar fighting to get out of his cocoon so he decided to help. He carefully cut away some of the folds so the butterfly could be free. He thought he was being kind and didn't want the butterfly to suffer. Unfortunately the butterfly didn't survive because just like in life, sometimes we needed the struggle so we can build the necessary muscles to fully develop our wings. It's the struggle that makes us strong, we just don't see the growth when we are stuck in the middle of the frustration.

A lesson in personal growth from Mother Nature

Another way to look at overcoming our blocks and achieving success is to look at Mother Nature. Once you plant that imaginary seed and decide to nourish the dream, you have to have faith and give it time to do its thing. Of course you have to develop good habits and cultivate the right environment. Plus it is helpful to be aware of our goals and take small actions every single day. If we do that our seed will begin to sprout and a small bit of personal growth will happen every day. We can't actually see the daily growth but one day we step back and wow, look at how much we have changed! We are starting to thrive!

Thriving is a great thing, but then as promised, the obstacles once again begin to appear. With all this nourishment and attention our growth doesn't stop. Like Mother Nature our lives silently and slowly continue to evolve. Our personal journey begins to get bigger and bigger. Eventually we start carrying a lot of dead weight. Life gets all tangled up and there is way too much energy spent in all the wrong places. That means it is time to trim some stuff from our lives. It is time for some serious pruning.

Growth is totally natural. It is the cycle of life. As humans all we need to do is have the courage to pick up the clippers and start chopping away. Yes that first cut may be difficult, but it really is for the best. We need to be careful and prune back only what is not working so we can open up our lives for another round of success.

The good news is, the next time our life becomes overgrown, it becomes easier to weed out the bad stuff. We now know where we want the growth to happen and we know where we need to trim. Pulling up the bad habits by the roots gets easier and we understand this has to be done before things get out of hand. We have hopefully learned to say "no" to the new sprouts that take our life in the wrong direction. Making cuts to things that no longer serve us becomes easier and easier. Soon we are thriving again and all those prickly thorns are now producing beautiful buds just waiting to blossom in the sun.

I couldn't end this motivational lesson without telling you about my tree that was the inspiration for this story. It all started with a leftover twig in a vase of flowers. When the flowers had wilted, the vase was carelessly put outside. I eventually came back to the vase and found that the two or three remaining twigs had

A White Hat & Rose Colored Glasses

started to root. I didn't want to let Mother Nature's efforts go to waste so I stuck the whole bundle of roots and twigs in the ground.

Little did I know that a tiny twig would quickly turn into one of the biggest, fastest growing trees I have ever seen - no kidding. That tree is only about six years old and this is the fourth time I have had cut it all the way back to the core. Plus I forgot to mention that there was no pre-planning when I planted the darn thing. The neighbor doesn't really like my tree because the enormous branches grow towards his side of the fence. The leaves grow so fast that by summertime they are so thick that they block the sun from the rose bushes. I'm also not sure that tall branches and overhead wires are a good mix. But what can I do? I have been part of its amazing transition from the beginning. I treasure this tree because I feel we have been on a personal growth journey together. All I can say now is, "Thank you Mother Nature for the inspiration." Growth happens!

Obstacles that may be blocking your path
Are you putting too much attention on...?

- **Problems.**
  People look for problems instead of putting energy into positive solutions

- **Fears.**
  Negative thoughts are stronger and more powerful than the positive ones

- **Judgment.**
  Like it or not the opinions of others do influence our decisions

- **Time.**
  Adults watch the clock instead of enjoying the now and taking time to smell the roses

- **Comfort.**
  New and different is frightening

- **The past.**
  Incidents from our past that prevent us from moving forward are where our limiting beliefs come from

- **Money.**
  Scarcity can be all consuming

Chapter 5

Resistance to Change:
What's the big deal? Change is simply doing something different

The resistance to change is a big reason people aren't living up to their potential. Yet change is the path to something better so I'm totally baffled as to why people are so unwilling to try new things or do things differently. Resistance to change holds such power in our lives but it is really nothing more than facing the unknown, and the adult mind has been brainwashed into believing that the unknown is full of scary things. Why? Because it all comes back to that protection instinct again, and safety is a huge issue in a grown-up world. That is what being an adult is all about, protection and safety. Mothers fiercely protect their young and fathers secure the home front and make sure their territory is well protected.

If that sounds sexist and out of date, you are probably right because like it or not things change. "Babe," "Honey", and "Darling" are no longer seen as terms of endearment in the work place. We say Happy Holidays instead of Merry Christmas and cigarettes are no longer advertised on television. Men have ponytails and earrings, tattoos are everywhere, and no one leaves their house without a phone.

Technology changes so fast that if I were to write about baby cams in our teddy bears or emergency operator buttons in our cars I would be behind the times before we go to print. Speaking of print, money is now mostly plastic not paper, books are digital, newspapers are for grandpa, and if it can be recycled it is.

Why do people get so excited about new technology anyway? It makes no sense (or cents) to buy a high powered, super-fast system that is equipped with all the gadgets if all you want to do is look at Facebook or send an email. And there are so many games available these days it is amazing that anyone ever gets any work done. Gone are the days of the joystick. The point is, change happens and if you don't at least attempt to engage in new ways of life you will end up feeling like you are riding a bicycle when everyone else is traveling by airplane.

Avoiding the unknown

Okay change is a part of life and we can't stop it, but why do we associate change with resistance and fear? If we don't know what is going to happen next that makes us uncomfortable. As I pointed out already, we look for all of the things that could go wrong. Our brains are trained to see danger first so when something new and different is presented we almost start to panic because the change is usually seen as something negative.

Yet this makes no logical sense whatsoever because the results could go either way. Things could be better, or they could be worse. We just don't know. Change is simply something new or different so why can't it be associated with all of the excitement and benefits that come with trying new things? The reason is that our protection mode is on automatic pilot so when we don't have all of the answers, we decide to be cautious. That means we resist change and decide not to take a chance at all. We talk ourselves out of potential success. We avoid the unknown and stay right where we are even though the reward of doing things differently could be huge. Our inaction keeps us in the painful place we are trying to get out of. Again, it makes no logical sense.

If we look at our childhood, back then everything was new and different. Hand a baby something new and they don't fear it. They don't associate it with all kinds of bad things. In fact they are curious and want to know more. So they pick up the unknown object, probably put it in their mouths and try to discover everything they can about this new object. They turn it upside down, sideways, and inside out if they could. Their minds are simply gathering data with no value attached to it. Soon they are bored with it and want something else new to play with. Of course this discovery process can be dangerous if it was a knife or poison, but that is why we are there to protect them from danger.

The point I am trying to make is that as adults we should know the difference between the dangerous and the unknown. Just because something is new and different doesn't mean it is going to kill us. Change may be a bit difficult or uncomfortable at first, but in reality, unknown things are very often good for us. Change can be exciting if you let it be, but too often we see a new object or method like an obstacle or a problem to be avoided. Doing things differently may take us off course or result in things we don't like, but it is doubtful that change will be hazardous to our health.

It just feels funny

Whether you see change as good or bad, one thing is for sure – change just feels funny! When we change anything, it feels odd. *Change is not comfortable, worn in, or well-rehearsed.* Change is awkward and often very uncomfortable. That is why we resist doing what needs to be done. We know we need to do things differently to move forward get out of our comfort zone but it's so darn hard. Our brains logically understand the needs and benefits of change but our instincts resist. New things could be dangerous so safe and comfortable is where we tend to linger.

When we finally do find the courage to take that leap of faith and change our old habits or learn something new, our bodies immediately resist. Change is an awkward feeling that makes our heart race where fear can easily take over and even lead to panic. We don't really like the unknown because it can make us feel vulnerable and out of place. Change is a good thing and we know we will get used to it but grown-ups too often let the strange new feelings get the better of us. The result is that we turn around and reach for our security blanket exactly where we left it.

In the long run change usually produces better results. Yes it is uncomfortable, yes it feels funny, and yes it can create tons of fear. The good news is that there is one simple solution to overcoming your fear of change… it's called practice. If you practice the new behavior those scary awkward feelings will soon feel natural and the positive results will begin to show. Then it will be time for another lesson and the whole thing will start all over again. Change just feels funny so accept it – don't run from it.

> Practicing the small stuff leads to success with the big stuff

Our comfort zone

Let's talk about two quick examples about the power of our comfort zones. First, why do we get so totally flustered when someone sits in our place at a dinner table, in class or at a business meeting? What is the big deal? Someone is doing nothing more than changing positions and sitting in a different seat. And technically it's not our seat. It's just a chair and anyone is free to sit there. Yet if you have a regular space that you claim as yours, hearts can go into panic mode if someone else decides to change things around and sit in your chair. That is your seat, your comfort zone, and changing that should never be allowed. So I challenge you if you dare, the next time you are at a meeting or in class, switch to a different seat after the break. Or better yet, sit in someone else's favorite chair. Push the boundaries and do something outside your comfort zone.

Or how about this one? One time I tried to help a friend by dusting for her when she broke her leg. Some help I was. She just couldn't stop herself. After I was finished dusting, she hobbled around in her cast and had to reposition every trinket and knick-knack in the entire place. This one goes one centimeter to the left, this one needs to be just a bit closer to the front, and this one just touches the edge of the wall.

People are so stubborn about change and that just goes to show you just how much resistance there is to doing things differently. Change means stepping out of our comfort zone and sometimes that is just too much to ask. Our comfort zones are almost sacred.

Get in the groove

I recently attended a golf clinic and the thing that stuck with me the most was a lesson about not changing things. This golf pro explained that before every tournament he goes out to the course forty-five minutes before his starting time. Not forty-six or forty-four. But forty-five. He explains that he spends ten minutes in the driving range, fifteen minutes putting, etc. He knows exactly how he spends every second of his time before he tees off. That way he doesn't have to think about any of it. It's all automatic. If a fan wants an autograph, or there is a discussion with his caddy, he doesn't have to panic or even stress because he knows where he has to be and how much time he can spare. Everything is on auto-pilot. The routine is so comfortable that all of his brain power is freed up to think about the competition.

So the question we must investigate now is "What in your life is working for you?" What routines are so good, and in-line with your goal that you don't dare change a thing? Then what routines are you still doing that no longer serve you? Do you have habits that have become ruts so deep that you struggle to get out?

Once you begin to see your patterns and become aware of your routines then it becomes easier to accept the need for change. Bad habits have a way of sneaking up on you. We ignore them or pretend that they are not doing any damage until they become so comfortable that they become like the golfer's forty-five minute routine. The bad habit is now automatic. That means it is time to change the way we do things and start working on new habits until it feels right. Keep what is working and change what is not. Doing something different can produce amazing results so stop relying on bad habits and try something new.

Remodeling your life

Another way to look at conquering your resistance to change is to think of it as remodeling your life. Life changes and that means things get worn out, broken, cluttered, useless, or simply out of style. Therefore when things in your life are not working or need to be upgraded it is time for a remodel.

I have a bright idea!

Susan Sherbert

And that was all it took to turn a relatively peaceful life into absolute chaos. So what was this bright idea? Green. The very color of trees and grass. The color of limes, leaves, and lettuce. Green is a fine color but the minute you commit to change anything, even the color of your walls, things will never be the same.

In order to have a beautifully redecorated life, you must first go through an absolute mess to get there. Change is messy and seems to splat everywhere. That means your old life will be out of commission for quite a while. Other aspects of your life may also be out of order because you need to use your energy for the endless supplies and new skill you will need to complete the job. Friends and family could get pulled into the mess as well and when that happens, forget it! Don't fight it. You may have to wear old clothes, order take out, and forget about extra sleep for a while. But eventually, one day all of this remodeling will be over and you will have the life of your dreams.

Okay, well maybe not the life of your dreams because dreams don't show uneven walls, drips of paint, cracks in the moldings, or rusty nails hastily painted over. You didn't mean for it to end up that way. You intended to do a fantastic job. You thought you covered all your bases and you were so careful with all your planning and preparation.

But then human nature kicks in and in this age of non-existent attention spans, things start to get a little tiresome. I mean by the time you have done all the prep work, and put two new coats of knowledge into your brain, who has time to worry about the color of the trim? Every living thing in the house has had enough and you just want the hell away from the mess.

Eventually you get there and things are fantastic... yet changing just one area of your life is never enough! It's just like eating a potato chip. You can't just leave it alone. Change the color on the walls and you need to buy new curtains. Next to a fresh coat of paint the floor begins to look pretty dirty so you decide you need new carpet. When the furniture goes back in, you notice how worn the sofa is so you have to go out and buy new furniture. The cycle only seems to end when you finally put your foot down and realize that you need to sit back and actually enjoy the beautifully remodeled life you have been creating.

I moved my couch

Here is another story that may seem a bit off track but trust me, there is a really good lesson attached. I'm sure you have heard of feng shui, which is the Chinese system of harmonizing objects with the surrounding environment. Now before I simplify this ancient art of creating good energy in your surroundings down to my simplistic childlike thinking, I must digress. I must tell you that I have total respect for the practice. Why? Because one day a house guest had left her feng shui book open on our table. I looked down and saw a picture of money being flushed down a toilet. This totally grabbed my attention because at the time I was very aware of money issues since my printing business was struggling.

Anyway, the book said that you must keep your toilet lids down because the open seat is like a funnel of energy just waiting to suck your money right down the drain. Humm, did I believe that, I'm not sure. Then the next day I went into the office and noticed that both toilets were commercial grade and didn't have lids. Now that is interesting. A couple of new lids won't break the bank. Maybe there is something to this feng shui stuff who knows. I have nothing to lose, so what the heck! That evening I went out and bought two new toilet seats with lids.

I didn't tell anyone what I had done, but for the next few weeks, I made a point of keeping the lids closed. And guess what?

Susan Sherbert

Within a few weeks we gained a new account that improved business for years to come.

Do I believe in the powers of the feng shui now? I'm still not one hundred percent sure, but here is why I think the ancient ways do get results. Let's say you are looking for ways to improve your relationship skills so someone suggests you move your couch to a new location with better energy. Simply because the furniture has been moved brings the desired results to your attention. You notice the sofa every time you go into the room and then you remember why you moved it in the first place; because you want a better love life. Change makes you more alert and shifts your focus and that awareness is a powerful benefit of change.

Chapter 6
Is the Risk Worth It?
The choices we have to make

Cooking the octopus

I never know where I will find my ideas but the other day when I was having a debate about a television show I just knew that conversation would end up in this book. It's that whole awareness thing. I was looking for material for my book, so the idea found me, but I digress. Anyway, here are some insights about taking risks that I found from a television show.

We were watching one of these cooking competition shows and one contestant didn't like seafood at all. She was terrified of it because as a child she stepped on an octopus. Now I find those eight slimy tentacles embedded with little sucker feet pretty gross when the creature is on display in the supermarket, so I can't image the fear when one grabs on to a limb and starts squirting black ink.

Seafood was a big issue so I have to give the contestant credit because she faced her fears. She tasted the fish, cooked a halibut, and even killed a live lobster. Kudos to her. Of course she was competing for a big chunk of money, but still it took a lot of courage to confront things that she had been avoiding for years.

A White Hat & Rose Colored Glasses

Life is funny that way because her determination got her into the finale. It was down to two contestants. Then the instructor suggested something very bold. He suggested that she cook octopus for her first course in the showdown. Wow! What a choice to make! My friend and I had a great discussion about her decision and I have to admit we couldn't agree. I thought it was brilliant! Get rid of those fears once and for all! Take the risk. Go big or go home!

My friend had the total opposite reaction. Play it safe! Octopus is very hard to cook and can easily become extremely chewy. Obviously the lady doesn't have much experience cooking seafood let alone something as touchy as octopus. It is just too much of a risk. The lady came this far and there is a lot of money on the line. If she chose something more within her comfort zone she will have a better chance to win. Besides, she did say she could really use that money. My friend continued to defend her position that cooking the octopus would be a bad decision.

Me, I still thought the idea was a good way to go. If she cooked it right, she would be sure to win, and even if it did turn out chewy, there were still two other courses to be judged on. If she chose to cook the octopus, yes, she may lose the competition, but to come this close to defeating her fears and then decide to run away at the last minute is not a courageous thing to do. Yet there is also the issue of the money. To me in my rose colored glasses way of thinking, no amount of cash is worth overcoming a fear that has followed you around for years. Once you defeat a blockage that has been holding you back, you will then be ready and free to accomplish even greater things, and that kind of victory is priceless.

In the end, the lady decided to cook the octopus. She overcame her fear, won the competition and received a big fat check.

Susan Sherbert

Failure isn't so bad

Failure is a huge block for many of us. It is often the foundation of a limiting belief that keeps us stuck. In fact failure has so much impact that we will be discussing the fear of failure again later. For this chapter we will look at failure in the context of the choices we make and risks we take.

Those darn rose colored glasses are in place again because I see many good qualities associated with failure. When you fail at something that means you made the decision to take action. You went for it! Be proud of that! Don't beat yourself up afterwards; it's not the end of the world. Think of failure more in terms of an obstacle than a problem. Our first attempt didn't work but other opportunities are on the way so dust yourself off and be ready for the next round. Besides, when you win two out of three, you come out victorious. You can fail and still win.

> WHEN YOU FAIL AT SOMETHING THAT MEANS YOU MADE THE DECISION TO TAKE ACTION

Failure is good because you have to practice getting it wrong until you figure out how to get it right, but you can't do that if you believe your efforts were for nothing. There are lessons in what went wrong. If you learned something then the experience had value. Thomas Edison said:

"Many of life's failures are people who did not realize how close they were to success when they gave up. Our greatest weakness lies in giving up. The most certain way to succeed is always to try just one more time. *I* have not failed. I've just found 10,000 ways that won't work."

A White Hat & Rose Colored Glasses

Are you closed-minded and don't even know it?

The other day I was telling someone my scary jellybean story. You may remember it. It's where I ask grown-ups to take a jellybean but they are unwilling to do so because there was one bad flavor in the bowl. The full story is on my website FunHappyEnjoy.com so stop on by and check it out.

Anyway, this friend asked a really good question. Why are people so unwilling to do something different when the down side is almost zero? I never understand why people are so closed-minded, so fearful, so resistant, and set in their ways for no good reason! There is an entire bowl of yummy-flavored candies but you won't take one because you don't want to risk getting a bad flavor. What's the big deal? If you try it and don't like it you politely spit it out in a napkin. No damage done - a drink of water and you are back to normal. Yet so many people are so stubborn, so closed-minded that they won't even try something new.

Food is a great example, and I'm not talking about eating crickets or anything gross. I'm talking about trying something that is simply prepared a bit different. Yet people still won't do it. This happens with so many other things as well. A while ago I woke up one morning with a sore back. I never have back problems! But this one was bad - three weeks of missed golf bad. Then one night a friend said she rubs onion on her foot to stop leg cramps. I thought why not try it? That night I cut an onion in half and rubbed it on my back. The next morning the back spasm was gone! Totally gone!

Now when someone mentions a bad back I tell that story and I am astounded at just how many people won't even try it! What is the downside? What are you afraid of? Okay maybe you smell a bit stinky and have to wash the sheets, yet way too many people refuse to try an onion even though they are in pain. Again, why?

I think it is because our negative thoughts have become so dominant in our lives. The immediate and automatic assumption is it won't work. Period, end of story. Even when there is little or no downside, people don't want to be disappointed if it doesn't work. They get so stuck in their discomfort that they resist change and can't accept, or even see, a positive outcome to their problem.

Oh, and by the way, I heard that the reason onions work on muscle spasms is because onions are full of potassium and the juice absorbs quickly into the skin.

OPEN YOUR MIND AND ALLOW THE POSSIBILITY OF GOOD THINGS TO COME INTO YOUR LIFE.

One bad grape

I'm reminded of the saying about one bad grape spoiling the whole bunch, or something like that. This chapter is all about the decisions we make. How can we make better choices and be confident about them if we think one bad idea or one negative possibility is the only outcome? Yes there is a risk and you may end up with an outcome you don't like, but why would anyone put that much belief into one possibility?

It's like never setting a toe in the ocean because there are sharks out there. The odds are against you being bit by a shark, hit by lightning, or getting the scary flavored jellybean. The risk is very small, but our resistance can be huge because the negative possibility has so much weight, so much fear, that people aren't easily willing to take a chance. We laser focus on the negative choices and we don't even see the thousands of other good grapes on the vine. If one is bad, they must all be bad. Don't let one bad grape spoil the entire crop and don't let one bad decision keep you from success.

A White Hat & Rose Colored Glasses

WHEN YOU ONLY SEE THE NEGATIVE POSSIBILITIES, HOW CAN YOU MAKE GOOD DECISIONS?

The least you could do is try another grape. Take that small risk and hopefully this time you will be wrong. Maybe the whole bunch really is worth eating. If you are making decision based on false data, or only one variable then no wonder you are stuck. Be honest, are you closed-minded and don't even see it? The next time you are asked to try something you are unfamiliar with, put on your white hat, face the unknown and say YES. You don't have to like it, and it may not work as promised, but try it anyway. When life presents you with a flavorful bowl of grapes, jellybeans or opportunities, do you join in? Do you embrace the unknown and try it? Or do you let your fears win and wrap yourself in your security blanket and stay within your comfort zone? A mental attitude that is failure focused leads to a limiting belief that it won't work or can't be done. When you only see the negative possibilities, how can you make good decisions!

Confidence verses doubt

As you examine your options and contemplate how to proceed, your frame of mind is also something to consider. If you are confident and believe in your choices then taking action isn't so scary. However if you doubt your decisions it becomes easier for defeat to find its way in. I remember a late night conversation with a friend where he once said that he truly admired my confidence. I was a bit perplexed. I have insecurities and doubts just like everyone else. Then he pointed out something I did understand. He said that if he is making a plan and someone questions his choices, he begins to doubt his decision. He goes back and reviews his options and wonders if he is doing the right thing.

Susan Sherbert

That helped me understand his comment about my confidence and I think my positive belief has to do with my outlook on failure. Before I make a decision I try to gather as much data as possible. I often ask for other people's opinions. I always tell them that I value their input but it doesn't mean I have to agree with it. I simply want the data so that I can make the best-informed decision possible, so I can make my decision. Since every decision I make is ultimately my responsibility I want to make it a good choice. *I take ownership of my choices therefore when I take action I have confidence in my decisions.*

If things don't happen the way I wanted, oops I was wrong. I made a mistake, a boo boo, a miscalculation. Obviously there were things I didn't see or didn't get right, but I made the choice based on the best input I had at the time. If I had different data or had the benefit of hindsight, of course I would have done things differently. But when I decide to take action, I make the best choices I can from the information I have and that gives me confidence. I don't question my decisions, I learn from them. I ask how could I do better next time?

Now let's shift from confidence to doubt. One day I was playing cards with some friends and we began discussing how the round played out and how we could have played it differently. This was all positive feedback until a friend said, "I threw out that card because I play expecting to lose." What? Why on earth would anyone do anything with the expectation of losing? I was surprised at that statement because I always expect to win. It could be a business proposal, a game of cards, or even buying a raffle ticket. If I make a choice to play, I might as well decide to win.

Some people may call that arrogance but I disagree. I see it as confidence or lack of doubt. My attitude isn't of superiority or that I am better than anyone else. It's simply about the fact that I automatically assume that I am going to win. If I don't, that's okay. The disappointment lasts for five seconds and I'm on to the next thing. My childlike thinking simply means that if I expect to win then I am not focusing on the failure. It's a bit like the sports technique where you are never ever supposed to say *don't miss*. You are supposed to focus on what you want instead of what you don't. For me, it truly is that simple.

I DON'T QUESTION MY DECISIONS, I LEARN FROM THEM

If you failed that means...

- You took action
- You had the courage to try
- You need more practice
- You just missed your target
- One idea didn't work
- You know what went wrong
- You may need some help

If you failed it does NOT mean...

- You are defeated
- You are wrong
- You lost
- You are rejected

Susan Sherbert

My short sheeting a bed adventure

Did you know that I sold 4,000 copies of a funny little book I wrote about short sheeting a bed? Well after that last story there is a chance you already think I am arrogant or that I am bragging, but the story could help move you into action so I'm going to take the risk and tell it anyway.

Honestly, I have no idea why I wrote a book about short sheeting a bed. It started out as a list of fun things for the kids to do when some friends came out for a visit. It ended up as 28 pages about a classical prank where you can't get into bed because the sheets have been folded in such a way that your feet get stuck. The book also talks about revenge, and how you can't short sheet a teenager's bed because they never make their beds in the first place. Anyway for whatever reason, I had written a book. Plus I worked in a print shop so formatting it and getting it into print wasn't that difficult.

But now what? Decision time. I could print a few for family to read and let my efforts end up in a drawer, which happens too often or I could do something with it. But again, what? I was stuck until someone suggested I send a copy to a bedding and linen company. Not a bad idea, but I just couldn't see a small 28 page self-published book sitting on a retail store shelf. I wasn't ready to give up so I decided to investigate a bit further.

Once again, the brain will present answers, but you have to be willing to receive the gift. I had a crazy idea for a promotional use of the book so instead of squashing the idea with reasons why it won't work and letting a dream wither away to nothing, I decided to take action. I made a phone call. That was it, one phone call. One action.

Okay, my mind is spinning and things are getting scary now. I have the name and address of the person in the marketing

A White Hat & Rose Colored Glasses

department of a major bedding and linen chain. Do I risk continuing on? There are all kinds of reasons as to why this idea will never work. Who is every going to go for a crazy idea of using a book about short sheeting a bed as a promotional product? Besides, I'm not a publisher. Heck I'm not even a writer! This is all just too silly.

But for some reason, I didn't listen to those little voices in my head. As I looked at the name of the marketing person, I thought, why not? What is the downside? She could say no…but she could also say yes. I could feel the resistance and the fear, but there was no logical reason for it. The risk is basically zero. I can print one copy of the book for a few bucks and the cost of a stamp I can handle. So what is the problem? There were no problems, only fear.

All I have to do is take action. Put the idea in a letter and send it out. How simple is that? It's easy, anyone can do it. So I made a 2nd choice to try something outside of my comfort zone. I wrote a one page letter explaining that my funny little book would make a good promotional product for college kids going back to school. Maybe use it as a free gift with purchase or something like that. Whew! Letter done, in the mail.

There were no problems, only fear

I truly didn't expect much, and I saw the whole lesson as nothing more than an exercise in facing my fears and taking risks. You can imagine my absolute total shock when two weeks later I answered the phone and it was the lady from the linen company. They loved the idea and wanted 2,000 copies to be used as a free gift with $50 purchase. Wow! Shock! Risk. Reward.

It doesn't matter that I was lucky, or that my timing was good, or that things like that just don't happen in real life. The only thing that matters is that I took the risk and made the choice to send out that letter. That one decision made me a published author. It put me on the path of where I am right now with this book. That one crazy idea followed up by a simple action was unknowingly one of the most direction-changing decisions of my life.

I have to add, there were plenty of obstacles attached. I wasn't a businessperson at the time so I had no finance experience to help me with costs, expenses, profit margins, etc. Plus they wanted invoices and packing slips. Luckily I had some graphic background so I was able to figure out how to create those. Then there was the shipping. They wanted the shipment split between stores and I never realized how big and bulky 2,000 books could be. There were boxes and shipping labels everywhere! And just to add to the illusion of my arrogance - let me tell you that they ordered another 2,000 copies the following year.

ONE DECISION COMBINED WITH ONE ACTION, CAN CHANGE YOUR PATH FOREVER

Mom and Dad

When talking about taking risks the conversation wouldn't be complete without mom and dad. Moms play it safe. Dads take risks. Yeah, yeah I know that's a broad assumption and doesn't apply to every parent, but we cannot deny that the lessons we learned from our parents have influence in our lives. I would hope so, otherwise what were all the sacrifices for! Why would a parent put that much energy into a child if they didn't want to help their offspring be happy and have a good life. Sometimes the parents get it right and sometimes they miss the mark but isn't the basic role of a parent to educate their child so they can make good choices in life? Mom and Dad do the best they can and then it is up to the child to make their own choices and live with the results of their decisions.

A White Hat & Rose Colored Glasses

Right now, let's assume that Mom and Dad each did their part and taught us how to make good choices. But which parent do we listen to? It's a bit like those little guys who sit on your shoulder whispering "Do it," "No don't do it." You can hear your mother's voice "Be careful. Don't do that, you might get hurt." Then your dad's voice responds, "Oh don't listen to her, go for it. It will be fun." It reminds me of this internet photo I found. Mothers and fathers are different. That is just the way it is so of course they are going to think and act differently. Neither side is good or bad, right or wrong. It's simply a different point of view.

Hopefully you find this photo funny but I can't control how you feel or react so on with another golf related story about the differences between men and women. One year I got talked into running on a charity golf tournament and couldn't understand why so few women wanted to play in these events. I discovered that because the tournaments are a bit pricey, women don't really want to spend that much money to "play." In addition they have to take a day off work so they think that their time and money could be better spent on other things. The time or money didn't bother the men. They would plunk down the cash to play in a tournament without giving it a second thought. They saw it as an opportunity to network and connect, plus a day away from the office was considered money well spent. Also there is a competitive nature to the tournament. Men tend to enjoy the challenge whereas the women get intimidated and want it to be fun instead of competitive.

Of course these are all generalizations, but the point is that there is a lot of data that goes into making a decision. Choices can be based on knowledge from anywhere - a mom, a dad, a coach, a teacher, or even ideas from this book. We are all different and every single action we take is based on our unique thoughts, feelings, and knowledge that we have acquired along the way.

A large majority of time our decisions come from reactions based on outdated information and subconscious data. Actions that have hurt us in the past are filed away in a location that tells us if this happens again, don't think about it just react, only react faster next time. Again, fight or flight; when we are scared we are programmed to run first and think second. Certain information gets stored in the automatic reactive part of our unthinking brain. Feelings that have caused us pain in the past are now programmed to bypass the logical, conscious part of our mind. These subconscious reactions are why I am nagging you about all this awareness stuff.

We need to bring some of our choices up to the surface so we can become fully awake and aware of the thoughts and feelings that influence our actions. Our success depends on it. It doesn't matter if our choices are influenced by mom or dad. It doesn't matter if we decide to take a risk or play it safe. What is important is that every choice we make matters! The more we can become aware of the reasons behind our decisions, the more we will make better decisions in the future.

EVERY CHOICE WE MAKE MATTERS!

Chapter 7
Fear of Judgment:
The emotions and feelings that hold us back

Emotions are not logical. You can try to talk some sense into your feelings but they seem to have a mind of their own. It's like they have superpowers that take over your mental capacity and do what in the heck they want. Logic verses emotion is a constant battle and the only tool that seems to create some sense of order is awareness.

Awareness is why I love the idea of my rose colored glasses. Because to me, when you can change your vision, or see the things you need to see, it brings awareness. That awareness leads to clarity. Once you can "see" the thoughts and feelings that are causing unwanted actions, then you can begin to change them. Then you will gain a better understanding as to why you do some of the silly things you do. It is not until you become fully aware of both your thoughts and feelings that you are finally able to get them to work together so you can change your actions and achieve the results you want.

Sticks and stones

"Sticks and stones may break my bones but words will never hurt me!" Are you kidding? Words are huge obstacles to face and the negative emotions attached can be deadly, and what makes it even worse is that far too often the damage is internal. Emotional injuries can easily get infected and spread quickly if we don't control the damaging thoughts in our head. *We* cultivate mind viruses and give them the fuel they need to stay alive.

Our bodies can heal wounds and broken bones without us having to think about it. When a physical injury occurs, an army is mobilized and our cells get to work repairing the damage. Our natural defenses don't need knowledge or permission to get started. Our body just does its thing because it automatically knows what needs to be done. However when there is emotional damage or we think we have been hurt in some way, there is no medical system or scientific process to repair that damage.

Even more troublesome is that one small injury could fester until it becomes a major limiting belief. It is up to our brains to figure out how to repair emotional damage but it doesn't have the magical healing powers that the physical body does. Our mind fixes what it can but if the injury is too painful or too hard to reach the brain takes a very logical approach. It buries the feelings so they can't do anymore damage.

Unaware of your fears

It surprises me every time I ask a group of grown-ups if anyone is afraid of fun. No one ever raises their hand. It's not like they are intentionally lying or anything - it's just that people are too often unaware of their fears.

For example, if I ask someone in the group to wear a funny hat and maybe sing a song, most of them tend to resist. Why? They just said they weren't afraid to have fun? But silly hats can be embarrassing and we all know that public speaking is a major fear so singing outside of the shower can be frightening.

Caution and danger are part of life but the fear of judgment seems to be among our most common blocks. The only reason I can think of as to why grown-ups don't skip is that they are afraid of what other people think. What else could it be? Skipping makes you feel happy. It's fun and carefree. When adults feel exciting moments of positive emotions, they are reluctant to embrace the feelings and skip down the street with glee. Skipping is seen as childish and embarrassing to many, so our joyous moments and feel good actions are repressed because of the fear of judgment from others.

Something else to mention is that when it comes to a choice between joy and fear, fear will win most of the time because we handle negative emotions differently. Negative thoughts and feelings have a lot of pull. They have tremendous influence over our actions. It is easier to give in to the fear than it is to stand up and embrace the joy. Like it or not, you have to work a lot harder to clear out the bad stuff. Negativity is very sticky and likes to hang on tight whereas the good stuff is a bit on the slippery side. It can easily slip away and out of reach without us even realizing the joy is gone.

No one wants to be a loser

Winning is good, really good, but that shouldn't mean that losing is bad. Just because we didn't win doesn't make us a loser or a failure. Or does it! Fear of failure is so strong in society that it seems that we have learned to associate losing with being wrong. If we don't get it right we feel like it's our fault. We feel like a loser. No wonder we are so scared of failing! Who would want to try anything if we feel that we will be condemned for our efforts, if being wrong is *wrong!*

A White Hat & Rose Colored Glasses

Society is all about the win, but we need to remember that it is okay to lose. Winning may feel good and positive but there are more valuable lessons that come from failure. Defeat may mean we need more practice. Losing could simply be a matter of luck or that someone else just had a better day. *Failure does not make you a loser but, unfortunately it can sure make you feel like one.*

Looking at it again, I think I have just discovered why there is so much fear associated with failure; losing is emotional! It hurts. *Failure is not really about what other people think of us - failure is about what we think about ourselves.* We put our valuable time and energy into something and if we don't win or our ideas don't get picked, we feel rejected. No one wanted us. It's like being the last kid standing in the playground. Rejection feels awful.

Whoa! That is a reason to be afraid. Now losing or failure is about feeling unwanted and unloved. That sounds just terrifying. We weren't only wrong but no one wants us and that can lead down a really bad path full of guilt, insecurities, doubts, and unworthiness. Failure I can handle. I tried and it didn't work so no big deal. Try again. But rejection is downright frightening.

The fear is not about failure, it's about rejection

Now that we know that failure is associated with rejection, how in the heck are we supposed to handle those intense emotions? We are not kids anymore and we can't have a tantrum because we messed up. Tantrums are bad sportsmanship, and can you imagine what life would be like if adults threw fits in the office, or if parents started to cry when they didn't get their own way? This is difficult for many adults because part of being a grown-up is learning to control our emotions and reacting in an appropriate manner. Yet the insecurity and doubt is there. It feels like we messed up and that our failure was really, really bad.

Adults are not very good with their emotions. Logically we

know we are not failures, but the defeat feels very personal so how are we supposed to handle our emotions. The result is that we learn to avoid the feelings associated with failure at all cost. That means we simply cannot try again. We avoid risks or don't take chances because another rejection is just too painful.

Why didn't they call me back?

To help prevent the fear of failure from holding us back we need to look at our failures and disappointments more like mistakes and simple errors. Being wrong is not the emotional failure we make it out to be. When we make a mistake, or our ideas are not chosen, it is not a rejection or a harsh judgment. It's not personal. It may sure feel that way, but the fact is, the harsh emotions we attach to rejection hardly ever fully concern us. We attribute all kinds of thoughts and feelings to other people when the chances are they aren't thinking about us at all.

When we were kids we were unaware of our surroundings. When we had something to say, we thought the world should stop and everyone should listen. As babies if we cried, we got attention. If we laughed, we got attention. If we were awake, we received attention. With all that attention, discovering that we are not the center of this world can be hard. It's like when we make a phone call and people don't call us back. There could be a hundred reasons someone doesn't return our call, but we think it's all about us.

Questions like that lead to uncertainty and that can result in some very imaginative responses. Most of the time adults can't come up with a single idea for a big, bold dream, yet simple situations like when someone did not call them back creates stories of extreme proportions. They must not like me. Maybe I was too pushy. I wonder if they are using another vendor. What did I do wrong! All of these are very creative responses, but why all the negativity? Why take one simple idea and spin it into complex tales of woe? We have no idea what someone is thinking, and even if we could read minds we would most likely find that the person isn't thinking about us one bit. The chances are the person didn't call you back because they have other things going on in their life. They got busy. The timing isn't right. You are only one tiny piece of the project and they are waiting for other information. I'm sorry to tell you this, but you are just not the center of their attention. It's that simple.

It reminds me of the advice I like to give people when they are going on a first date. They are full of anxiety and apprehension with all kinds of crazy thoughts in their heads, but why? It's not like we are committing to marry the person, and we are not even obligated to see the person again in the future. Besides isn't that why you go on a date in the first place; so you can get more information and learn more about the person? Again, why all the complications and drama?

Adults try to analyze other people's thoughts. Before they even get to know a person they try to decide if there is a potential fit for a long-term commitment. Would this person fit in with our family? Are they honest and someone I could trust? I wonder what their plans are for the future.

Or how about when we are about to go into a meeting or party? Before we open the door to enter we often have moments of anxiety or self-doubt. Am I dressed okay? Will I fit in? Am I going to say something stupid? Imagine if we as grown-ups could simply accept the moment with no judgment or projections. No stories as to why someone didn't call us back, no images of us getting it wrong. It doesn't matter if it's a first date, a simple phone call, or a business meeting. Try to eliminate expectations, fears, and judgment. Think of the experience as a play date where it's nothing personal.

Stop turning a single event or conversation into something it's not. There really is no need to complicate things with added emotions and negative stories. If we focus on the things that matter, the things we can control, everything else will either get in alignment or get out of the way. Suddenly, life becomes easier. Once you understand that it's not about you, the situation quiets down and you feel better. I know there is a lot more that could be said on the subject but that would only get in the way of the message. Keep it simple. It's not personal. What more needs to be said.

I'm so happy I could cry!

To lighten things up, let me ask you a silly question. If we are not allowed to show hurt or fear then why do adults cry when they are happy? Crying is only something that we are supposed to do when we are truly sad? And you never see little kids spilling tears of joy? So what changes the way we express our emotions as we get older?

I'm sure there must be some scientific reason for our tears of happiness, but I have a theory of my own. As kids we used to express our emotions with passion in energetic ways. As grow-ups we learn to filter and suppress our emotions both the good and the bad. We were told to use our indoor voice because it is unacceptable to get too excited in the house. We eventually discovered that our actions have the power to make other people feel sad. As a child we were praised and encouraged as we learn to walk and talk. Then once we got those skills all figured out, we were then told to stop whining, stop crying, and stop fidgeting.

Maybe crying tears of joy is because we aren't allowed to cry when we are sad, hurt or angry. Only "babies" cry when they lose or get hurt. For whatever reason, adults are not allowed to boldly express their emotions in public. As we get older we learn that the carefree anything goes emotions of childhood have no place in our grown-up life. And it only gets worse. We learn to control our anger and hide our fears. We try not to cry in pubic even when we are scared or think our heart is breaking. As for hugs, kisses, and other displays of public affection, boy can that get us in real trouble!

As kids emotions were not a problem, but as grown-ups emotions are a difficult element to handle. Therefore, it is my theory that since we are not "allowed" to jump for joy, cuddle our loved ones in public, or acknowledge our fear of being rejected, our emotions simply leak out of our eyes. We cry when we are happy because it is acceptable to do so. Thank goodness someone hasn't decided that tears of joy have to go into hiding too.

Emotions are part of being a human. Why we feel we must contain them with such strict rules I will never understand. So for now we are stuck with tears of happiness and I'm okay with that. Heck I'll take tears of joy any day because it's a whole lot better than having emotions come out our nose.

Up the middle, down the middle

Another reason why trying to predict other people's thoughts is a bad idea is because everyone is different. Even if you found the best chocolate in the world and had solid evidence that it could prevent cancer (or some other terrible illness) some people would not be interested. Do you remember the old saying that you can't sell chocolate to vanilla lovers? In fact, did you know that vanilla is the best-selling flavor of ice cream? Just because I like chocolate doesn't mean *everyone else does*. Maybe the person is diabetic. Maybe they are allergic. Maybe they prefer strawberry to chocolate. Everyone is different so go out and find the people who love chocolate and you will have much better results.

People can be the same in many ways but we also have to remember that people are different. The other day one of my golf buddies said "Great shot! Right *up* the middle!" at the same time I said, "Alright! Straight *down* the middle!" Both of us knew the hit was good, and our responses were the same, but different. The exact same thing can be drastically different from person to person. One person may find jumping out of an airplane to be fun, but others would find it terrifying. Different is not good or bad. It's not wrong, or right. It's just different!

A stumbling block that may be holding us back from obtaining the things we want is that we forget to see the value in being different. Other people live on this planet and these people have feelings and needs that aren't always the same as ours. Unfortunately we are more like sheep, where we go with the flow and assume everyone thinks the same way. We look around to see what others are doing so that we can verify that we are on track. Sometimes that can be good because feedback is helpful. However if you start comparing yourself to others then it can lead down a dangerous path towards doubt, panic, or defeat.

The reason these comparisons are so dangerous is, again, because everyone is different. We are all motivated by different things so if a person is doing better or ahead of us, that does not mean we are not making our own progress. It does not mean that we are behind or doing something wrong. All it tells us is that they are in a different place at that moment. Comparisons are never what they seem. It reminds me of a when a person messes up a routine or flubs a presentation. A friend says, "Don't worry you are really not that bad." Then when someone is really good and just nails it, the friend could also say, "That was great, but you are really not *that* good."

A White Hat & Rose Colored Glasses

Sometimes it is all good and sometimes we struggle. The point is, we are all on our own different path. Don't assume we are all heading in the same direction at the same time. When our roads cross it is good to have companionship on the journey, but when your path heads off in a different direction, we need to be true to ourselves and take the road that leads us where we want to go.

Journey of the Month

I have no idea why we connect with the people we call friends. There is one pal who is so opposite it baffles me as to why we are friends. But instead of fighting our differences we decided to embrace our individuality. We came up with a really great idea. We started what we called the journey of the month. The rules were simple. One person (the planner) chose an outing and the other person (the guest) had to simply show up and fully participate for a minimum of two hours. They had to be open and accepting of whatever the journey happened to be.

The guest was not told a*nything* about the outing beforehand, not even what to wear. All they knew was what time the planner would pick them up. Since we were both so opposite, the idea was that we wanted the other person to experience something different. But not just half-heartily try it to please the other person.

We wanted an outing with no expectations, no judgment, no resistance, and no fear. Show up fully and experience whatever happens. One thing that we both found odd was that the planner was the person that became anxious. Did I pick a good journey? Will she like it? How will my friend react? The person that just had to show up was totally fine. They had to accept whatever was presented to them so they didn't worry about it. They were not allowed to engage in judgment, or resistance. That meant they had nothing to fear.

Susan Sherbert

I was the guest for our first journey. Remember, I was told nothing. When I got in the car I had absolutely no idea where we were going. We drove for a bit and I didn't recognize anything. I didn't really even try to guess because I was focusing on the now and willing to be open to anything. It's all good. So I was absolutely and totally amazed when we pulled up in front of a church.

Okay this was interesting. I am spiritual, but I'm not religious, and religion is such a very personal thing. That means this journey had some risk on the planners part, yet a promise is a promise. I said I would be open to anything so there I was boldly walking into church with my friend. The experience was a good one and I know if she had asked me to go to church I would have refused. I would have stuck to what I know and what is comfortable for me, yet for those few hours we both enjoyed freely sharing our differences with no judgment, only acceptance.

On to planning her journey! Church was important to her and she wanted to share her experience with me but my first thought was to resist trying to top our last journey. I wanted to be true to our mission and give her an experience she wouldn't otherwise have had. And she was right, being on the planning end of this adventure was a lot more stressful then just showing up and being open to anything.

About a month later I picked her up and we drove to a local mall. I'm not much of a shopper so buying something was not our intention. It wasn't until I opened the door to the Color Me Mine that she understood what she was about to experience. We were going to paint some pottery. Neither of us are the arts and crafts type, but I like to play and have fun and I always wanted to try the place so that was why we ended up there.

To me the adventure was all about having fun and being creative. But I will never forget the first words out of her mouth. "I am not creative. I will be terrible at this." Right then I knew it was the right choice. Her resistance was that she didn't feel that she was good enough and to me that is the perfect reason to try it. It's about enjoying the process not the outcome. The important thing was the time spent together painting and creating regardless of the outcome.

Again a promise is a promise so she was open and willing to participate. We picked out our pieces, sat down and began painting. Neither of us knew what we were doing but the experience was what counts. I have to admit that our finished pieces were really not very pretty, but every time I look at my spotty, patchy, oddly colored spoon rest, I think of that day and am thankful that we shared the experience and embraced our differences.

You just never know

Life is unpredictable and full of the unknown and that can be rather uncomfortable. It's a scary thought not knowing how our efforts will be received. I've just taken pieces of my life and opened it up for the whole world to see. Will people really like this book or will they just tell me it's good to be polite? Will anyone even bother to take the time to read these pages? And what about my social media efforts? Will my work get re-posted around the globe or will it end up ignored or in the recycle bin? I have no idea because I haven't figured out how the popularity contest of life works yet.

When you do anything in life, you can never truly predict the success or failure of your efforts. People are different. Conditions change and it is almost impossible to see all of the variables that come into play. Look at the dot com businesses when they first got started. People were so sure that any company with a website would be a huge success that they were willing to invest big money in anything ending in dot com. But life is strange and unpredictable so nothing went according to plan.

Susan Sherbert

I remember a marketing class where they talked about a campaign for pets.com or something like that. The advertising gimmick was a talking sock puppet. The instructor asked the class about the company. Yeah, of course everyone in the room remembered the sock puppet commercials. Then he asked how many people ordered a product from the company. Only one person in the room actually ordered from the website, and even then the purchase was for less than twenty-five dollars. A big success and a big failure. Life is unpredictable. It's full of obstacles and fears. And you truly never really know how it will turn out. All you can do is keep on trying and never ever give up.

Just who is it that decides the success or failure of a product or company anyway? How come everyone seems to use Google? What's wrong with dogpile.com! And could anyone have predicted the success of a pet rock or the popularity of the *Rocky Horror Picture Show*? And why is bottled water a hundred billion dollar industry when you can get water from the tap for free?

What about cat videos? Why does a cat playing in a box get a million views while my video about short sheeting a bed can hardly get a hundred people to click on it? And why not dogs? They do silly things too. As for those reality television stars, how can a good looking drunk make a fortune while a well-trained critically acclaimed actor struggles to find a part?

Life makes no logical sense. It's unpredictable and honestly it's just not fair. I have no idea why some things take off while other really great ideas fall flat. Why do some people love us and while others can be mean and critical? Life can be difficult but it can be pretty wonderful too. The way I see it is, you really only have two choices. *Take action and try; or do nothing and accept defeat.* The possibilities are unpredictable but that could lead to some really good things. My advice. Try on a pair of rose colored glasses and see what happens.

Life just might surprise you.

PART THREE

Taking Action And Wearing The White Hat

Hopefully your imagination has kicked in and you have found a little spark or seed that will inspire your big bold dream. And my childlike thinking is sure that your rose colored glasses are helping you see the things that you need to see.

Now it is time to take action! I encourage you to put on the good guy white hat and let your newfound inspiration move you into action. Your passion and purpose are within your reach, you just have to find your confidence so you have the courage to live, dream, and enjoy.

Chapter 8

Truth:
Be honest, especially with yourself

If you have a desire to transform your life and live your dreams, then it is time to become the hero in your own life. It is time to put on that symbolic good guy white hat because to me a white hat represents the old fashioned hero. These people are honest, trustworthy, and sincere. They stand up for what is right and they don't run or hide from the truth. They have honor, courage and integrity. Good guys do the things that need to be done and they tell the truth.

I realize my image of the good guy is idealistic and not total reality but why can't we strive to live up to something that good and hope to have a life that grand! Of course we will fail, mess up, and make bad choices because being a hero is extremely difficult. But the point is if we want a better life then we must live a better life. And that means we had better get used to the truth.

> IF WE WANT A BETTER LIFE, THEN WE MUST LIVE A BETTER LIFE

A White Hat & Rose Colored Glasses

To tell the truth

If I had to pick a single trait that makes up the characteristics of our hero, I would say it all comes down to the truth. The truth is super important and a major piece of the foundation for the white hat. The truth is all about facts and reality yet those are different depending on the person, culture, or situation. The truth is hard to explain, yet somehow we all internally understand what the truth is, what our truth is.

Scholars have been debating the idea of truth for years and they still can't agree on the meaning. Truth is being honest and being honest is telling the truth. It reminds me of the catch 22 where you go round and round in circles getting nowhere. What am I supposed to do if I can't describe the truth? I have an entire chapter to write on the subject. Since I struggle to describe what the truth is, then maybe we should look at what the truth is not. It makes sense because when we are not being truthful, we know it. Lies, falsehoods, deception, misleading information, cheating, or even little things like avoidance and omission are all a result of not telling the truth.

It seems so simple to be honest but telling simple lies makes life so much easier. If you are asked to do something outside your comfort zone, it's easier to tell people that you are busy than to admit that you are scared. If a loved one asks your opinion and you know they are not going to be happy with your answer, a little white lie isn't so bad. Even admitting when you are wrong or made a mistake is hard to respond to with the truth.

To me, everything comes down to being honest. If you are not seeing the real facts of a situation your path is likely to be unclear. If you are telling lies, or if people are telling you lies, even with good intentions, the damage is often far worse than if you spoke the truth in the first place. I mean, how can you fix a problem if you are not aware there is a problem in the first place? Where there is deception there is likely going to be trouble.

White Hat Awareness
If you are not truthful, especially with yourself, there is likely going to be trouble

People lie

People lie. Life is not fair. There is evil in the world. That is the truth. But the purpose of this book is to help balance our view of life. We need to see the positive side of life as well as the negative and understand that good and bad coexist. This can be hard to believe at times because when life is bad, it appears so awful, painful, and frightening that we can hardly see anything but the negative. Yet the positive does exist. I recently saw one of those inspiring quotes on social media and the message really stuck with me.

> "People will let you down, welcome to life... People will also lift you up, save you, love you, embrace you, teach you, and guide you. Welcome to life!"
>
> —Elle Febbo

The truth is super important but it is a good guy trait that is also extremely difficult to achieve. Not only do we lie to others to prevent hurt feelings or cover up our mistakes, but we lie to ourselves. We just can't help it. If you say you are going to get up at seven but hit the snooze a few times and don't actually get out of bed until seven-thirty that's a lie. We promise to quit smoking and then give in and have a cigarette. Everyone makes promises they can't keep when it comes to diets and New Year's resolutions. The truth is people lie.

Oh wait there's more! What about all of the lies that we never actually "tell" but think instead. I'm no good. I'm a lousy partner. I'm stupid. I'm not worthy. And the biggest one of all; I can't. These are all lies too, but sometimes we believe them. If you are human, you lie. If you are human you make mistakes. If you are human you also do a hundred other really great things that you never give yourself credit for, probably because you are too busy focusing on the lies, mistakes, and untruths. And that is exactly why I believe the truth is so darn important. If you would just tell the truth and admit when you are wrong or make a mistake, then you would be free to move on and get to the good stuff.

Lies are bad, the truth is good. We know that. Isn't that one of the first lessons we learned in childhood. So what happened? Telling or hearing the truth can be difficult and a lie can be a quick easy fix. Making excuses, avoidance, and fibs are certainly easier ways to go but if we are not careful the lies and negativity can take over the focus of our lives. My hope is that you begin to seek out the truth in spite of the discomfort and fear. Welcome the honesty of others and begin to uncover some of the uncomfortable feelings you have been avoiding. Your life can change once you learn to become conscious and aware of when you are telling lies. When you confront your mistakes and acknowledge your fears it opens your life up so good things may enter. Awareness is my idea of the truth.

White Hat Awareness
Awareness is my idea of the truth

Susan Sherbert

The truth is uncomfortable

The truth is supposed be a good positive trait, so why do we spend so much time and energy avoiding it! We tell little white lies to spare hurt feelings all the time, and even worse, we lie to ourselves. Why is the truth so difficult? Maybe it is because the truth can be very uncomfortable. If we tell the truth, we could get in trouble. If we tell the truth we could hurt someone. If we see our own truth we may have to admit that we were wrong. The truth is uncomfortable.

It can also be healing, empowering, and free us from a lot of negative thoughts and feelings. As humans we care about people so we lie to protect them from the emotional pain. Too often this does more damage than good because whatever the problem is it still exists. Lies rarely fix things, they only hide or delay the emotions.

It's a bit like sweeping dirt under a rug. The issue is still there. The lie only covers it up so no one can see it. Whatever it is that we try to hide behind the lie will be waiting for us to be dealt with sometime in the future. Seeing at least some of the dirt is a good thing. You need to be aware of what is causing you damage so you can figure out how to repair it. Covering it up or pretending the truth doesn't exist is not helpful in the long run.

I think this could be why rose colored glasses have gotten a bad reputation. People tend to associate them with blinders that help avoid the truth. This encourages people to see the illusions created by the avoidance or the lie. I am trying to change that because I believe rose colored glasses should help you see the whole uncomfortable truth problems and all. You should be able to see the good and the bad. That means you see the dirt under the rug but you also see a lot of positive solutions to fixing whatever is causing all that pain. My hope is that people use the tinted lenses

A White Hat & Rose Colored Glasses

to help see the truth instead of hiding from it. Rose colored glasses should enhance your vision not block it.

I understand that life is much more complicated than simply being honest, but if we don't deal with what makes us uncomfortable, it will continue to block our path, get in our way, and make things worse. Lies complicate things. The truth should be simple. However when we don't want to face our own problems or have those difficult conversations with others, we avoid the negative emotions by telling a lie. That only adds more negativity to the situation. Become the hero in your own life by seeing the truth that you need to see and by having the courage to face the uncomfortable situations you would rather avoid. Truth requires courage.

More often than not it's the person telling the truth that struggles. Being honest means we may upset people, add to their problems, or get someone in trouble. We know the truth could possibly help, but our words could also hurt. This is especially the case if we are trying to point out something someone is not ready to hear.

My philosophy is to try to have honest conversations quickly and get them over with! How many times have we stressed and worried, almost making ourselves sick simply because we were ignoring the need to acknowledge and discuss an important issue. Then when we found the courage to speak our mind, the conversation wasn't as difficult as we imagined.

I remember this one time when I was looking after my aunt and uncle. It was a rather difficult situation because my uncle was blind with Parkinson's and my aunt was his devoted wife and lifelong caregiver. One night my uncle confided in me that before he died, he wanted to go to Scotland to visit his brother. That was fantastic, except my elderly aunt had a bad heart and couldn't fly. That means my disabled uncle would have to make the trip without her - and she would never go for that!

Susan Sherbert

"The conversation wasn't as difficult as we had imagined!"

Our family discussed all of the possibilities and looked at all of our options… but how are we ever going to get my faithful aunt to agree? We could get a friend to fly over with my good natured uncle, and he would be well looked after once he got there, but who is going to tell my aunt about the trip? We can't ask her to be separated from her husband. They have been together for as long as we can remember.

For weeks, the family avoided bringing up the subject of the trip. No one wanted to tell my aunt that her loving husband wanted to travel to Scotland. How in the world would we ever get this tiny old lady to agree to something like that? Then one day I realized it was simply time have that difficult conversation we had been avoiding and stressing over for weeks. I gathered up my courage, explained the situation, and had an open and honest conversation. And do you know what my devoted caregiving aunt said? Her response was, "His passport is in the top dresser drawer."

Apparently she truly loved her husband but she was getting old and was just plain tired. She would never complain, but she could really use a break from the responsibilities of looking after him for all these years. Thankfully this truthful conversation ended in happily ever after! Of course not all conversations end that way, but the question really is, "Why is giving honest feedback so uncomfortable?" Our family wanted to do something that would mean a lot to my uncle, but we didn't want to hurt my aunt's feelings or make her life more complicated. Luckily I had that tough conversation because in the end all of my worries and concerns were just that, *my* worries and concerns.

A White Hat & Rose Colored Glasses

White Hat Awareness

BEING HONEST HELPS US SEE THE WHOLE UNCOMFORTABLE TRUTH PROBLEMS AND ALL

How you doing?

Let me tell you one of my biggest pet peeves and hopefully by the end of the story you will see the lesson I'm trying to get across. I just hate it when people, virtual strangers, ask me "How you doing?" That question makes me cringe. It sounds like fingernails on a chalkboard to me! Why? Because the guy at the grocery checkout doesn't really want to know how I am feeling - so why ask!

Or even worse, I've heard listeners calling in to a television show and the first words out of their mouths are "Hi Ellen, how you doing?" Like she is going to tell a caller and a million other listeners that she is having a bad day, or that she is worried because her dog is sick. Even if she is having a fantastic day, she doesn't have time to answer that question in detail. It's not a simple yes or no answer. How you are doing requires an explanation and the person asking should have the time to listen to the response or they shouldn't be asking the question.

The whole thing is just so ridiculous to me, and that dang "how you doing" phrase has become a standard greeting in our society. In fact I was asked that three times within an hour or so last night. Everyone says it. But not me! Why do I find those three words so irritating? Because if you ask me how I am doing I'm going to tell you! If I'm having a bad day I'm not going to lie and say I am fine when I am not! Why would you put people in a situation where you are almost required to lie? That one simple question has forced us to become a society of liars. I'm fine. I'm good. I'm okay. Everyone is not fine all the time! There are days when we are truly having a bad frustrating, horrible day, yet people automatically respond, "I'm fine." Liar Liar your pants are on fire.

You may not even be consciously aware of that dread question but I am super sensitive to it and I refuse to get sucked into a dishonest response! That means when people ask me how I am doing, I am ready with my automatic reply. Usually I just say 'Hi" or instead of telling lies, I simply wait in silence for just a second or two. By then they have already moved on because people don't honestly wait for an answer anyway. However if I am having a bad day I often respond, "Don't ask," and sometimes I'm sure the person never even noticed that I didn't respond with the expected, "I'm fine."

I know all this may sound pretty stupid, or even crazy, but I truly don't like to lie, and I really get irritated when untruths become a subconscious habit. Do me a favor and tomorrow or the next day make a point to pay careful attention to just how many times you automatically respond to that how you doing question. You just may be surprised at the amount of lies that you are subconsciously telling.

White Hat Awareness
UNTRUTHS CAN EASILY BECOME A SUBCONSCIOUS HABIT

Say what needs to be said

The other day a group of us were talking about a movie we had seen. My best friend and I both rolled our eyes and started to express our negative opinions about how stupid the story line was. It was so bad that we couldn't even finish watching the entire film, yet it won an Academy Award. Totally ridiculous! Then I

A White Hat & Rose Colored Glasses

turned to another friend and asked her opinion. What a position I had just put her in! Of course she was never going to say that she enjoyed the film after we had just totally trashed it. So what was she supposed to say? She did exactly what was expected and said something about it being okay. In other words, she lied.

The incident got me thinking. My friend and I were both telling the truth and expressing our opinions about the movie, however we made it very intimidating for someone else to express a different opinion. We put the other person in an awkward position so of course she was not going to express her true opinions - just agree and keep the peace. It was a casual social setting so why would she want to make waves and have to defend her views? She probably should have had the courage to say she loved the film but remember all that talk about keeping us safe and letting fear and negativity win? She didn't know us that well and she certainly didn't know how everyone else around her would react. Her instinct was that her opinions could cause her trouble or pain - so she played it safe. She told a little white lie.

It is so unfortunate because far too often we are untrue to ourselves. We give in and agree or tell people what they want to hear because that is the easy way to go. We lie to keep the peace because if we express our opinions the results are unknown. We don't know how people will react. I only hope that these lessons help people become more conscious of their tiny untruths so their first instinct is to tell the truth and express their opinion. Tell a white lie if you must, but make it a conscious choice to do so.

The whole thing makes about as much sense as what I call the "Barry Manilow Syndrome." For some odd reason people seem to resist publicly admitting that they are a Barry fan. Yet if no one is a Barry Manilow fan then how in the heck does he manage to sell songs and fill up concerts year after year? Not bad for a man no one seems to like. The point is, you have opinions, preferences, likes and dislikes. You are free to express your opinions and tell people the truth even if you disagree with them. If you are a Barry fan, be proud of that. Make telling the truth and expressing your opinions your automatic response. Telling lies happens, but lies should make you feel uncomfortable!

White Hat Awareness
TELL A WHITE LIE IF YOU MUST, BUT MAKE IT A CONSCIOUS CHOICE

A promise is a promise

Responsibly is also a very strong white hat hero trait because *I see responsibility as the truth in action.* What I mean by that is when we keep our promises and do what we say we are going to do, we are turning our words into positive action. We are living the truth, not just talking about it. When we keep our commitments we are choosing right over wrong, and when someone is responsible, a lie never enters into the equation.

People who are heroes keep their promises. Following through and being true to your word builds respect. It is also one of the biggest differences between success and failure and the super successful people take this to the extreme. Their "nothing can stop me" mentality is based on one thing, being true to their word. Once a commitment has been made these people fulfill their promises. If they say it, they do it. They are among the few who say they are going to call you back and actually do. If they decide to lose twenty pounds before a big event, they accomplish that too.

These movers and shakers accomplish great things because they make a decision and accept nothing less. They are true to their word and do what they promise whether it becomes difficult or not. If they get a better offer, they still choose to honor their word and fulfill their obligation. If they decide to get a role in a film, or become president of their company they don't make excuses, or accept defeat. They just get it done. And you can be pretty darn sure that these mega successful people keep the promises they make, especially the ones they make to themselves. If they say they are going to get out of bed at 5:02, they are up by 5:01.

Obviously we are not all that responsible or that successful all the time. However you are responsible for your own actions so if you say it, then you must do it. This is not an easy thing to do and there are very few of us who can be so truthful that we keep every promise we make. However wouldn't we have more success in our lives if we were true to our word, took more responsibility for our mistakes, and reduced our lies and broken promises? Of course! *The more responsible and truthful we are with our actions, the better our lives will become.* Notice I said truthful with our actions. Remember, people lie and the mega successful people are no exception. That means the message we should be paying attention to here is the importance of keeping our promises and following through with our actions. Keeping a promise and telling a lie are two completely different concepts.

White Hat Awareness
If you say it, you must do it

Responsibility

A good example about responsibility that stuck with me came from John Travolta. When he was being interviewed he said something about how he tries very hard to keep within a film's budget. What? Am I hearing that right? He is John Travolta! He has tons of money plus as a superstar he doesn't have to worry about things like budgets, does he? Other people are responsible for those details.

Well I suppose there is a reason John Travolta is one of those mega successful people because as the interview continued I realized that he is one of those people that keeps his word. The lesson I learned from that interview is that even with his vast wealth, John Travolta is responsible and stays within budget. When he makes a film, there is a contract that says I will do this work for this pay. The budget could be five dollars or five million; the amount is irrelevant. When there is a goal, a budget, or a plan, responsible people will try to honor it and not disregard it.

Budgets are not just for the corporate world either. The idea really inspired me so now when we plan parties, vacations, or even trips to the grocery story I try to have some kind of budget in mind. It may be an extravagant budget or a very tight one but to me having a realistic target to work with helps maintain focus. Plus it is a responsible and fair way to go especially if there are other people involved. Having a budget is like making a promise or commitment, a way of saying I will do this work for this reward and hopefully everyone will honor their part. This doesn't always happen, and things always change, but at least with a budget there is a foundation to work from. I think budgets bring a very powerful awareness to a project because if you agree to do something then you should keep your word. If John Travolta has a budget, why can't you, on a smaller scale of course?

White Hat Awareness
WHEN THERE IS A GOAL, A BUDGET, OR A PLAN, HONOR IT. DON'T DISREGARD IT

A White Hat & Rose Colored Glasses

Excuses! Excuses!

Now let's shift from responsible to irresponsible. To me making excuses is a very unproductive and irresponsible trait to have. It is certainly not a trait you want to master if you plan to wear the good guy white hat. In fact, excuses are habits full of misleading behaviors, avoidances, or omissions.

People who make excuses have a potentially destructive way of thinking because they don't want to take responsibility for their own actions and poor decisions. We have talked about people making mistakes, messing up and doing dumb things. That is okay. That is human. The negative outcome of our action is rarely the real problem. The bigger issue is how we accept or deny our contribution to the mishap or disaster.

People who make excuses think it is always someone else's fault. They make up stories, point fingers and shift the blame to anyone but themselves. It's my parents fault. The teacher is an idiot. The boss is out to get me. The government should be responsible for that. It wasn't me. Someone else made me do it. These sound like anyone you know? Of course! We all have excuse makers in our lives. And my guess is that they are not among the most successful and supportive people in your life.

Excuses are the shifting of responsibility and a way of deflecting or at least softening the impact of a negative action or poor decision. This only perpetuates the bad decisions because if it wasn't your fault, then how can you learn from your mistake? What I am trying to say is that there is nothing positive about making excuses. Sometimes there are good honest explanations for a mishap or a negative action, but hopefully you take responsibility for your part. Excuses are the stories we tell so we don't have to accept the responsibility for our actions.

Susan Sherbert

White Hat Awareness
An excuse is the story people tell to avoid responsibility

Why all the guilt?

Before I begin here I should probably be honest and mention that this section may be a little bit biased. Why? Because I am not a big fan of guilt. I just don't see the point in all of the negative doubt, and harsh feelings attached to a mistake. Guilt is something I am not intimately acquainted with. That being the case, hopefully my white hat awareness lesson is still something you can relate to, if not I won't take it personally.

Let's begin by getting in touch with all of that imagination we talked about earlier. Wow, doesn't that first chapter seem like such a long time ago? Anyway, imagine you are in a court of law and you are on trial for whatever the latest "crime" you happen to be feeling guilty about. You stand in front of the judge and he/she reads the description of the crime, injustice, bad decision, poor judgment, or miscalculation that you are accusing yourself of. Remember you are on the stand so you can't explain, justify or make excuses. You simply have to enter a plea. What will it be? Guilty or Not Guilty?

If the "crime" you committed is true and you are guilty as charged, then take responsibility for your mistake. Pay the fine, apologize to the victim, and do the community service your inner imaginary judge requests. Accept the verdict and be done with it. You entered a plea of guilty and accepted the consequences of your actions so quit dragging out your sentence. Stop spending unnecessary negative thoughts on something that you already settled. And while you are at it, since it is your court, your rules, why not seal the record, and stamp a big Case Closed sign on the file just to be sure.

I realize this may sound a bit silly, but to me, so does all of the brain power people waste on such an unproductive emotion as guilt. And it gets even worse because let's say the plea you entered was not guilty! That means you were innocent of all wrong doings and committed no crime at all. If that is the case then what is there to feel guilty about? You were innocent.

Okay, so maybe the situation didn't turn out as planned, and perhaps you made some errors in judgment, or didn't have all the facts, but that doesn't mean you are guilty. Getting something wrong, failing, and honest mistakes are all grounds for disappointment, but not guilt! If you are not guilty then stop treating yourself like you are a prisoner in your own mind. Your imaginary jury looked at all of the facts and couldn't find enough evidence to convict let alone waste time and energy on a trial. The evidence supports a not guilty decision then who are you to argue. Not guilty means not guilty. You are innocent of the crime and cleared of all charges. You are free to go so have faith in your own imaginary internal justice system and accept your verdict!

White hat Awareness

IF YOU ARE GUILTY, ACCEPT RESPONSIBILITY. IF YOU ARE INNOCENT THERE IS NOTHING TO FEEL GUILTY ABOUT

Lies should be uncomfortable

I started this chapter with the idea that the truth often makes us feel uncomfortable. We don't want to hurt other people's feelings or we don't want to cause trouble so we tell quick lies to make the person feel better and our discomfort goes away. From my perspective, once again, we are looking at it all backwards. Shouldn't telling the truth be easy and telling lies be the uncomfortable part? That makes total sense to me, however we tell little white lies all the time and never even notice or consider it a lie. How you doing - remember? The nature of not wanting to burden someone with our problems by saying we are fine when we are not is a totally acceptable thing to do. If it wasn't no one would get anything done because we would be too busy listening to everyone complain. No one wants that.

On the other hand telling nothing but the truth is a totally unrealistic way to go. It is so much easier and faster to tell a little white lie. Lies are a part of life. However, lies should be the exception not the rule. Plus when you do decide to tell a little white lie, it should feel a bit uncomfortable.

One of the reasons I feel strongly about this point is because like so many other things in life, once we become comfortable with something, it becomes easy and unconscious. We don't even have to think about it. Telling a lie is a very dangerous path to take.

Lies lead to more lies. Small untruths turn into blatant lies. The truth gets pushed further and further away so we can't even tell the difference any more. I remember an interview with the real Wolf of Wall Street guy and basically he said that when lies build up you begin to believe them. When that happens you can convince yourself that dishonesty and deception are not a bad thing.

I also remember talking with a friend who was going through a divorce. He was complaining about his wife. He was hurt that she didn't respect him. He said he just couldn't trust her anymore. I looked straight at him and said, "That's because you lie to her all the time." That kind of shocked him. I think he was at that point where the lies had become so comfortable, so common, that he wasn't even aware he was telling them anymore. In his mind they weren't lies, they had become just a way of life.

There are tons of things that make us feel uncomfortable and situations that we don't want to deal with. If something is blocking our path or getting in our way then wouldn't it be better if we hear the truth so we can fix it? Lies make us feel better but they do not lead to solutions, only more problems. Lies are even worse because they erode trust and trust is the foundation for so many positive things; strong relationships, good business, and of course our good guy hero who wears the white hat. Life's journeys don't usually start out full of deceit but tiny little lies and untruths can easily build up resulting in serious damage.

Remember how we discussed that negativity has more influence over the good stuff. Well when it comes to trusting people and telling the truth, negativity has tremendous power. If we are dishonest or fib even once, the distrust is there for a long time afterwards. It takes a lot of truths to make up for one little lie because the negative impact of a lie lingers. In fact lies are so powerful they have the ability to hurt people to the core. Small lies can do a lot of damage so let's turn things back around by getting more comfortable with telling the truth.

White Hat Awareness
Small lies do a lot of damage

White Hat Awareness for Truth

- If you want a better life, then you must live a better life
- If you are not truthful, there is likely going to be trouble
- Being honest helps us see the whole truth problems and all
- Awareness is my idea of the truth
- Untruths can easily become a subconscious habit
- Tell a white lie if you must, but make it a conscious choice
- If you say it, you must do it
- When there is a goal, budget, or plan, honor it. Don't disregard it
- An excuse is the story people tell to avoid responsibility
- If you are guilty, accept responsibility; If not – you are innocent so there is nothing to feel guilty about
- Small lies do a lot of damage

Chapter 9

Action:
The actions you take determine everything

Have you ever noticed that some people seem to make success look easy, while others sit around complaining? People who dream big and live a full life of passion and purpose don't hang around hoping that someone will hand them the solution they are looking for. The only difference between being the hero in your own life or staying right where you are is that the people who truly want something better take action and get their dreams started. Let me repeat that. The people who succeed get started! They take action. That's it.

Hopefully you are using rose colored glasses, have gained clarity, and are beginning to see your truth. You should also be aware of your positive desires as well as of some of the habits and beliefs that you want to change. But what good is a dream, a thought, or an inspiring lesson if the idea stays in your head? Now is the time to put all that thinking and awareness into action and get your dreams started.

A White Hat & Rose Colored Glasses

The importance of getting started

I didn't have all the ideas for this book before I began to write it. I had a rough vision and plenty of inspiring thoughts. One of the blocks so many people create is that they put off getting started because they want everything to be right, perfect, or in a logical order. It becomes almost a fear of commitment because they want to have all the pieces before they begin. This rarely works because in the beginning people rarely have all of the knowledge and skill they need to finish the task. You have to practice and make mistakes. You have to learn what works and what does not. It takes time to build your confidence and expertise. Besides, once you do get started everything is going to change anyway. New ideas will lead to bigger and better ideas and your project or journey will change, grow, and unfold as you go. The path to our goal is rarely a straight line.

When I started I had a jumbled mess of possibilities but I also knew that I had to just get started. I had to stop worrying, stop making excuses, and stop waiting for all the answers. I'm not even sure exactly where I began but once I got started the ideas quickly began to flow. And I am always surprised at just how many other ideas my brain comes up with *once I do get started*. One idea leads to another and the thoughts build on each other until you end up having to set aside some really good ideas because you have too much material to work with.

It's a bit like one of those really old cars. They had manual crank starters that took a lot of momentum to get going but once the engine fired up you could travel for miles. Trust your brain because your mind will take one idea or image and create great things from it. But you have to start! You must crank your engine and take action to get the ideas out of your head and into the universe.

Your mind resists this because doing something unfamiliar or unknown leads to fear and apprehension. Getting started can be uncomfortable or painful even. But very quickly the brain builds up strength, ideas start to flow and momentum starts to happen. You create that muscle memory and your new skills begin to become more comfortable. You now have some idea as to where you are going and even a small bit of positive reinforcement can be very motivating. Getting started gives you a direction. Soon you are in the groove, moving forward and getting stronger and more efficient every day.

Success, transformation, and even life happen layer by layer. Yet nothing can be built or achieved without that first initial layer being installed. You need a foundation to build on and that means getting started by taking that very first step or action.

White Hat Awareness
Get Started! Take that first step or action

Try putting it on automatic pilot

Remember the story about the golf pro who went out exactly forty-five minutes before every game? That idea stuck with me and soon after that I created a speaking engagement routine. I now start my talks with the exact same story every time. I know the story about the scary jellybean inside and out. I could tell it in my sleep. Of course I'm nervous before I speak and I realize that my talks don't always match what I had planned, but now when I get up to speak, I don't have to be nervous for those first few moments because I know what I am going to say. I know where to start.

If getting started is something that is holding you back, I

A White Hat & Rose Colored Glasses

encourage you to find one subject, idea, or action that you are comfortable with and start with that. You don't have to start at the beginning and you don't have to have all the answers, but you do have to begin somewhere. It may take practice and you may have to try your favorite skills out on family and friends, but take the best part of your plan or the idea that excites you most and start with that. Starting with that one action, topic, or subject that you know and like makes the whole process a bit more natural, automatic, and a little less frightening.

White Hat Awareness
Begin with something comfortable

Let your mind wander forward

If you are not living the life you want, a common reason could be that you are thinking too much about your past or immediate future. Remember the importance of your imagination and that itty bitty seed that will grow into your dreams? Well if you are stuck in practiced routines, memories of the past, and outdated thinking, that could be part of the problem. Our habitual thoughts and daily habits become a very comfortable thing. The results are predictable. We know the outcome. Adult brains like that because nice and comfortable is the easy way to go. So until you make that mental shift and let your mind wander forward to a vision where anything is possible, instead of restricting it with blinders of the past, you may continue to be stuck.

With that in mind let me ask an insightful question. What do you think about most of the time? My guess is that the majority of your thoughts and energy are focused on either the immediate present, things like your daily to do list, or activities and memories of the past. Now if you were seeing the world from a child's point of view, the majority of your thoughts would be different. Imagination, dreams, and anticipation of the future, is what makes up the spirit of childhood. Kids are focused on the future and they get excited about new things to come. Adults too often let those silly thought loops of the past take over so we end up not paying attention to either the future or the present. We allow unrelated thoughts to distract us and become oblivious to everything else.

I have this theory that we often don't see our purpose or vision because of that old 80/20 rule. In the business world it's where they say that eighty percent of your business comes from twenty percent of your clients. Or eighty percent of the work is done by twenty percent of the employees. When it comes to thinking about your life and finding that life-changing inspiration, I believe the 80/20 rule applies as well. Eighty percent of adult thoughts tend to be about the past or present, and only twenty percent or less of our mental energy goes to dreams of the future.

This is why it is important to keep an open mind and unlearn old habits. We need to flip those figures so that a much higher percentage of our thoughts are about things that have not happened yet. You need to educate your brain so it will get excited about a future full of success and possibility. Once you start building up images about your future, they will become part of your daily mind set and soon the seeds you have been looking for will begin to appear.

When we were young our peripheral vision was also vast so it took in every detail. We saw the whole picture instead of focusing in on only certain parts. With age our vision shrinks, and I'm not just talking about the need for reading glasses. They have done studies showing that we can lose up to half of our physical peripheral vision. Grown-up brains have learned to focus on only what we are looking for. It's like we shine a spotlight on the area we are working on and leave everything else in the dark. Kids see

A White Hat & Rose Colored Glasses

things adults miss all the time. How many times have we been totally amazed by an obvious observation that comes straight from the mouths of babes?

The good news is that these studies also show that with a bit of practice both our internal and external peripheral vision can be improved with practice. We just have to re-train our brains to start seeing the bigger picture again. Easier said than done; but at this stage it's all about awareness. We need to start with the present and learn to become aware of all that surrounds us. Then expand that vision and begin to see the larger picture - and hopefully that picture includes some really compelling images of your future!

My white hat lesson or suggestion is to begin by giving your future your full attention. Every single day, put some energy and thought into your dreams. Remember the adult word for imagination? Begin to visualize your future. Coaches and inspirational teachers often suggest the idea of making a vision board. The reason people find pictures helpful is because a collection of positive images about your future, your dreams, and your desires are the stories you want to keep in your head. You want to see your future every day.

Shifting to a future focused thought process can also be done by reading a mission statement daily, or by reviewing a list of goals. It doesn't matter what method you choose, all that is important is that every single day you put time, energy, and attention on the objects, feelings and events that you desire in the future. When you can connect your vision (or imagination) with thoughts of possibility, amazing and powerful things can happen.

White Hat Awareness
VISUALIZE YOUR FUTURE EVERY SINGLE DAY

Susan Sherbert

Never stop asking why

As kids, when we reach a certain age we discover the power of questions. And that is why we go through that annoying "why phase." Grown-ups may find the phase irritating but to a child why is vital. Answers are important because they not only give us the data we need to fill in the blanks, but our new information leads to more questions. When we are curious about the world around us we want to know more. And wanting more, even if it's just more knowledge, can be very motivating. It is our questions and our desire for answers that often lead us to some new and interesting places. Remember the guy who loves grass? He built a hugely successful career because he was curious about grass. And the odd thing is that once we start asking specific and detailed questions we never seem to run out of information. Curiosity seems endless and only leads us on a path of wanting to know more.

Some people refrain from taking that path because they are afraid of what they might find. Others don't go there because they never search for anything outside of their comfort zones. *If you have dreams and want more out of life, the best action you can take is to start asking questions.* Creativity and curiosity can lead you to place you never imagined before. Those three little letters W-H-Y have changed the world with innovation, improvements, and technology that could never have happened if someone didn't first become excited about exploring possible solutions to some rather interesting problems.

A fun example of this that I have always wondered about is gas. How did people discover Natural Gas in the first place? You can't see it, hold it, smell it, or even hear it so how in the heck did people figure out how to turn this invisible "stuff" into a major source of energy and heat. Add to the fact that with just a tiny

A White Hat & Rose Colored Glasses

little spark, it can cause a massive explosion. So why would anyone ever imagine that you could pipe this silent deadly invisible thing into homes all around the world. But if someone didn't ask "how," "why," or "what if" we would still be cooking over a campfire.

Asking questions and wanting to know more truly has changed the world we live in. So imagine how you could transform your own life if you simply started asking questions. You can have a big bold dream and achieve things you never thought possible but you must first become curious and start asking questions – really, really good questions.

White Hat Awareness
BECOME CURIOUS AND START ASKING REALLY GOOD QUESTIONS

Get the knowledge you need

This is kind of the "gotcha" part because once you start asking questions, you then have to start looking for the answers. Asking the right questions will put you on the path to bigger and better things, but those questions must then be followed up with actions. Now the action step you must take is to acquire the knowledge you need. Start searching for the answers to those amazing questions. If you are stuck or want something different out of life then you need to find the information required so that you can begin to answer your important questions.

Of course there is such vast knowledge in this world that no one person could know everything. Why then do we continue to struggle on and think we can do everything ourselves. Wouldn't it be so much easier to find a professional and use their expertise to help us avoid mistakes, progress faster, and get closer to our goals and dreams? The answer is obviously a yes, but too often we choose to take the hard route and try to go it alone.

If you are struggling in business, relationships, money or yes, even life, a good white hat action is to ask for help. If math and numbers are not your strong suite, admit your weakness and hire a bookkeeper, accountant or financial advisor. If you struggle with clutter and disorganization there are consultants for that. You may be strong in the creative areas and weak on the business side. Either take a class and learn new skills or find a partner or employee that has the expertise that you do not. Find the knowledge you need to fill in the gaps and improve the areas that are not your expertise.

You may know enough to get by, or you may be the most experienced person in your field, but there is so much available information that you could never take it all in – yet isn't that why we find an expert in the first place? They help us make sense of our questions and like so many things in life, small adjustments are often all that is needed. In the end it comes down to having the knowledge and understanding so that you can put your best ideas into action. Thank goodness for the professionals that have the knowledge we need because their answers help our success happen.

White Hat Awareness
FIND THE KNOWLEDGE YOU NEED BY ASKING FOR HELP

Start with baby steps

Once you finally start asking the right questions and gain the knowledge you need to move your dreams forward, you will become excited. Your new knowledge inspired some really great possibilities and you are committed to change. You are ready to jump in with both feet and you want big results now!

Yet that is exactly where things start to fall apart. Motivational workshops and books are very inspirational but they tend to have rather poor long term results. But it isn't the teacher, the coach, or the guru that failed you. It is simply the fact that you most likely jumped ahead, skipped a few steps and didn't take the time to start with the recommended baby steps.

This is so true with many things in life. When we get excited we want results now. We want to lose thirty pounds the first month or double our annual sales in thirty days. We want to be living our dreams right this very second. However this impatience is one of main reason we get off track; because we take short cuts. We want to jump ahead to the finish line and don't understand the value in all of those tiny little steps we must take to get there. Just strap on the jet pack and let's just get it done. Sorry to tell you this but big changes don't happen overnight. No matter how motivated we are, we must still start with all of those silly boring little baby steps.

You probably remember that my dream is to golf every golf course in my state. Well that also means I want to improve my golf game. To accomplish this I went in search of the knowledge I needed and found a golf pro. My instructor knows his stuff and his total focus is all about the impact position of the golf swing. In our first lesson he readjusted my grip, shifted my weight, and explained a whole lot of really insightful stuff. Then he gave me a lesson that started with small short swings that focused on feeling the proper impact of the ball on the club. So what did I do? Did I go out and practice the nice easy swing he showed me? Of course not.

I was excited. I want to smack the heck out of the ball. Isn't that why I'm taking these lessons? So after a few short swings, I went right back into that big full swing. But it was okay because

I was focusing on my weight shift, hand position, divots and all of the other things my pro taught me. I felt like I was doing everything right but for some reason my shots were not improving. I was getting tired of all this impact position stuff. I know I am building a strong foundation but I want to see progress now. Maybe I need to try even harder and swing a little faster.

No. The reality is that what I really needed to do was slow down, focus on the lessons I had been given and start with baby steps. Skipping the small details is so typical. How often do we rush to get to the good part, and don't take the necessary time to learn the important boring stuff that eventually builds a foundation that won't easily collapse? And we wonder why our short-term efforts don't achieve long-term results!

At the start of our next lesson my instructor saw my big full swing, and I could see him shaking his head. Then he patiently explained how important it was to warm up the hands, feel the connection with the ball, and start slow. We need to add another layer, another lesson, another thought reinforcement. He said all of the pros warm up with the small details first. They work up to the big swing because they know that they have to master the finer details, the small stuff first, before they can be successful at the entire game of golf.

It reminds me of a new salesperson. You would never send a rookie out to sell one of the biggest accounts. They start with the smallest clients first so they can practice and make mistakes. We all need to start with baby steps because that is how you build a strong foundation. The problem is those small baby steps aren't very exciting. They are super important, just not very fun.

Back to that darn impact position. I was a good girl and continued on with my baby steps even though I just couldn't see the improvement. I was looking for big results, I wanted to see real changes now so of course I couldn't see the improvement. Then it happened. Apparently my foundation was being built and

A White Hat & Rose Colored Glasses

I didn't even notice. One day my golf buddies said, "That swings sounds solid" and "You are really making good contact with the ball." That was all it took and I knew a strong foundation was in progress. I suppose the life lesson I have learned from these endless baby steps is not even about the importance of building a strong foundation. The lesson I think I have been learning is called patience.

White Hat Awareness
Practice the small stuff first! It will lead to bigger and better results!

Before I conclude this chapter on action, let me summarize with one last consideration. Finding clarity and then taking action on those powerful new thoughts are what we are trying to accomplish. So let me ask you this: What steps will you take today that will move you towards your vision or goal?

There is no substitute for action!

White Hat Tips for Action

- Get Started! Take that first step or action

- Visualize your future every single day

- Become curious and start asking really good questions

- Find the knowledge you need by asking for help

- Practice the small stuff first! It will lead to better results

- Begin with something comfortable

Chapter 10

Priorities:
Doing the right things

A big part of finding your passion and positive purpose begins by deciding what is important in your life. Hopefully by now you have removed some limiting beliefs and are starting to see some of your truths that you may have been avoiding. At the very least you should have some little spark of something you desire in your future, a possibility of things to come.

Now begin looking at the choices and actions you take in your daily life. What do you do every day? Evaluate your actions and begin to notice any distraction, responsibility, excuse, emotion, or even busy work that you currently spend time and energy on. By paying attention to what you are currently doing, you should begin to become aware of the activities that are not supporting your desires. What is getting in the way of what you really want from life?

At this point all we want to do is assess what we are spending our time on and begin asking ourselves why we took on that project, watched that program, offered to help, signed up for that committee, avoided the gym, etc. We are looking for hints as to why we have allowed our lives to get off track. What are the driving thoughts and emotions that are working and what areas do we need to change so our actions are in alignment with our priorities.

Change your focus and you will see new things

How many times have we given advice to someone we love trying to point out the reasons why they may be struggling or unhappy? We can clearly see their patterns and we know what their issues are but they will just not listen to us. And then one day our loved ones come to us all excited because someone else gave them the exact same advice we have been giving them for months or years even. Yet for some odd reason the outsider's advice is seen as the best thing in the world. Why had I never thought of that before they exclaim. We can only shake our heads in frustration and can't understand why our advice, the exact same message, had never sunk in before.

This happens all the time and I can't even come up with a really good reason as to why that is. The good news is that eventually awareness does happen. It is okay to be irritated that your advice was ignored while a stranger gets all the credit, but in the end all that really matters is that awareness and thought shifts happen.

Once new understanding takes hold our focus begins to change and that means our actions are likely to change as well. For example maybe a nice acquaintance pointed out that we like to date "bad boys" because we are rebelling against our parents. Wow I never thought of that before that. Now I get it. I understand the reasons for my choices and why I have been getting poor results. Now I can begin focusing on different things. Once you shift your focus, you will begin to a see hundreds of new and different choices you have been missing.

It is not until we have these light bulb moments that we begin to see other choices and open up to new ideas that we would never have considered before. Once our priorities change we are now receptive to other options that would have been automatically ruled out before we had our major thought shift. For another example, let's say someone pointed out that we are a very caring person. He suggests that we would make a really good nurse. Finally we see the value in our own gift and understand that an accounting office is not where we should be working.

Now that our awareness has been shifted, suddenly we start to see all kinds of possibilities we have been missing. There are tons of opportunities for good jobs in different fields but in the past we only saw what we were looking for - accounting related opportunities.

It reminds me of the reticular activator. Basically it's the scientific term for the part of the brain that stays on alert. We actually have an area in our brain that is programed to make you notice some things and ignore other things. Let's say you buy a pet turtle. Suddenly you begin to see turtle stuff everywhere. It's not that there are more turtle images in the world, it's just that you have shifted your focus so now you are aware of, and subconsciously look for, anything turtle related.

It makes sense because when my friend and I go out to places with crowds, we often we turn to each other and comment something like, did you notice all of the fathers with baby strollers? Sure enough that day we see tons of other dads with kids. Now it has almost become a game where we pick something out such as really tall men, really big purses, or even people in really tight pants and sure enough, we see lots of whatever it is we have decided is popular that day.

Becoming conscious of our desires and aware of our actions is important. What we look for, what shifts towards our conscious mind, will present itself. If you want to be a hero and wear a good guy white hat, simply shift your priorities so you are focusing on the good stuff that you want. It is time to really start looking at our lives and try to begin to see what areas are working well and what are not. Then cherish the good things and keep taking more of those positive actions. Put more of those kinds of activities on the top of your priority list. Once you start to look for things in alignment with what you want, the opportunities will begin to appear right before your very eyes.

White Hat Awareness
WHATEVER YOU MAKE A PRIORITY IS WHAT YOUR MIND WILL SEEK OUT

Squeaky wheel gets the grease

Now let's focus on what we are actually doing every day. Too many adults work long hours and add unnecessary stress and worry into their lives simply because they get sucked in the whirlwind of life. People respond to the tasks that make the most noise. It is like the old saying "The squeaky wheel gets the grease." But the question we all need to ask is; are we doing the right things? Is our time spent on the tasks that get us the results we want? Or are we exhausting ourselves responding to the things that demand our attention but are not really important or in line with our goals?

One of the biggest things we can do to change our ways and become the hero in our own lives is to get our priorities straight. Far too often we live in a reactive world where we continually grease that squeaky wheel and spend our limited time on activities that are not taking us in the right direction. Instead of working on our priorities, we are fighting fires and spending energy doing things that demand our attention.

Susan Sherbert

Things that squeak and make a lot of noise are generally what get done first. The items that would make the most difference in our lives, too often get pushed aside because they don't demand our immediate attention. And unfortunately it's usually the negative activities that seem to require immediate attention because it's that old fight or flight instinct once again. Negative things appear dangerous so we respond to them now, whereas the beneficial positive actions that we should be doing, are the ones that we feel we can push aside. We don't have time to organize and plan, gather more information, spend quality time with friends, or even relax and dream because there are too many things that are demanding our attention right now! Take action now and make the noise of that irritating squeak go away. Set your priorities straight and start producing results that are worthy of all the effort that you are taking.

When we are distracted by people and projects that are leading us astray or taking us in the wrong direction, it is only natural that we want to get rid of that noise! But wouldn't it be a better if we could replace the wheel that is causing the squeak? Don't reward distracting time suckers with a squirt of grease! Go out and get a new and improved wheel that will get you to your destination without all of the drama. Maybe we should rewrite that old saying to say, "The squeaky wheel gets *replaced*."

Being busy and living in a reactive world makes us very productive, but what is the end product that we are creating? Too often our actions produce a life where we run in circles with no joy, no fun, and nothing but movement. People are busy with lots of action, but the results of that action should not be more action. You should be riding on a strong and supportive foundation, not an old and creaky wheel that is hindering your progress. We should have positive results to show for all our effort.

A White Hat & Rose Colored Glasses

White Hat Awareness
Replace the squeaky wheel instead of greasing it with your attention

I hope you are staying busy

What is important in your life? We can't spend our days doing what we want because there is work to be done. Responsibility, work, time, and money are all major factors in the grown up world. Money must be made, there are things to buy, bills to be paid. As a result the exuberant ways of childhood decline, fun gets pushed aside, and our adult brains are rarely given the freedom to experience that worry-free, childlike joy.

On those infrequent occasions that we do allow ourselves to embrace our passions and lose ourselves in the now, our brains are finally given the opportunity to forget about all that stress and worry. That means for those rare moments, time and money become meaningless. We break out of our stress box and temporarily allow ourselves to indulge in the glory of now, leaving our anxieties and troubles temporarily behind.

So if time and/or money are a struggle for you or if you feel stuck and can't get out of that box of stress and frustration then you need to change your priorities so that your action will change. The reality is, if we stopped reacting and gave ourselves time to think, we would achieve our dreams so much faster. That is so difficult to do because we are busy. We need to keep moving and get things done. Work harder and faster. That seems like the best solution.

Where does our time go anyway? I'll tell you where it goes. It goes to sitting in traffic, being in meetings, and to downloading, uploading, or reloading information that you don't have time to handle. Sometimes computers seem to save us time, while other times computers seem like a big waste of time, but one thing for sure is that technology has changed our perception of time. A second is still a second, but in this click button world a second can also seem like forever. And how can time be exactly the same for every person on earth, yet be handled totally different by each one of us? Time is a strange thing indeed.

The other day someone said to me, "I hope you are staying busy!" and I had to stop and pause for thought. I'm not sure staying busy is actually a good thing. It would be nice to have time to relax and read a book, enjoy a leisurely stroll, or even sleep in. But that doesn't get things done. Even vacation times are often packed with activities so that only a small part of the agenda is set aside to relax. In our society it seems that if you are not busy then you must not be productive. Just look at our meager vacation time; how can you unwind and rejuvenate in only two weeks? And even then I read that one third of Americans don't take all of their vacation time!

It's unfortunate really because that statistic shows me that in this country, *we put more of a priority on working and staying busy then we do on enjoying ourselves.* We seem to value activity instead of rest. If you are not giving yourself space to slow down and enjoy your life then what I want to know is: what are you doing that is so important instead? Do you really want your priorities to be all about staying busy or are there other things that should have a higher significance in your life? Again, it's all about awareness, but we must first get out of that automatic don't think just keep going behavior. Become aware that you are creating the hectic schedules that you think you must follow.

If your life is full of nothing but busy, maybe this is one of those situations when you need to put on your rose colored glasses and really look at the actions you are taking. Ask yourself, "What am I spending all of my time doing? Am I feeding the squeaky wheel that is demanding my attention and putting aside the things that are important to me? Am I staying busy to avoid actions that make me feel uncomfortable? Do I put any importance on the things *I like* and enjoy?"

At least some of your actions should match your priorities so begin to truly look at what is meaningful and important in your life. Are you doing at least a few things that are in line with your values and passions? If not, slow down and take some "you" time to figure out how to change that. What actions need to stop, what thoughts need to shift, and what priorities must be moved to the top of your daily to do list?

These are the reflective conversations you should be having with yourself during your downtime. But wait, I don't have any downtime because I am too busy. Remembering your priorities and giving the important things your attention is why you must find even a small space of time to recharge, renew, and just breathe. Taking even a moment in the day to stop and let the mind wander off and rest is a wonderful thing. And we can't do that if we are continually busy. Heck even the President of the United States, who is extremely busy, takes some time off. If you don't have any time for what is important in your life then it is time to change your priorities.

White Hat Awareness
If it's important make it a priority

The emotion of now

One very important distinction between our carefree childhood and our adult reality is the impact of our negative emotions. Kids don't focus on the negative because it is the adults that take the responsibility to keep the children's world safe. The instinctual traits that protect us by being alert and watching out for the bad stuff hasn't developed yet. It is not until we grow up that our mind shifts from a world of carefree joy to a world where our brains are almost obsessed with protection. I mentioned it before but those things that have the potential to harm us, or our loved ones, hold the most power in our mind. Positive things are nice but when our brain thinks we are in trouble, danger and fear win every time.

Negative emotions elicit a quick response. That means when we are in danger, or think we are in danger, we must act now! We tend not to react forcefully and immediately to positive emotions because they are not a threat, therefore negative emotions get all the attention. We actually feel and remember more positive emotions but since the good feelings don't require an immediate action they don't always get the attention they deserve.

If we want to attract more positive results and maintain the visions of our future, then we need to give our good emotions time to develop and space to settle in. Confident thoughts and feelings need time to linger so they can attract more positive energy to start a celebration. We forget this because negative emotions demand an immediate action. It takes more of a conscious effort to attract and maintain happiness and joy into our lives. Don't let the negative emotions steal the show. Welcome the positive feelings and encourage them to stay a while.

Now imagine how quickly we could change the direction of our lives if we switched it around so a large portion of our thoughts were about positive possibilities! That is a powerful suggestion, but even to my childlike mind that is not very realistic. Adults have responsibilities that do not exist in childhood so adults must think differently. They must learn from the past, and do the things they don't want to do. That is called being a responsible adult.

A White Hat & Rose Colored Glasses

However, just because we live hectic lives doesn't mean we have to push all of our dreams aside. And that is exactly what too many adults do. They get so focused on the now that they totally forget to put any mental resources into the future. To help find the positive images that will challenge and inspire, you need to increase the amount of time you actually think about the good stuff.

White Hat Awareness
LET POSITIVE EMOTIONS LINGER BECAUSE THEY REQUIRE MORE TIME AND ATTENTION TO GROW

When time and money become meaningless

To me, what many grown-ups are lacking are those rare moments where nothing else matters. People say they want to have more but then they don't do anything about it. They continue on with work, stress, and worry. They think that they don't have time for fun yet, fun is important because when we are in those happy moments we almost transcend time. When we engage in positive actions we love, we let go of our fears and worries and lose ourselves in the pure energy of innocent fun and absolute joy. Our bodies feel the good vibrations they have been missing, craving even. We welcome the distraction because we temporarily have some breathing room to stretch out and enjoy. It is in those moments that our brains can relax and dream of our future. When we immerse ourselves in positive activities time and money no longer exist, and that feels pretty darn good.

On some level we know we need to make time for the things we enjoy yet we resist because we have too many demands on our time. Many adults struggle with letting go because they find they can't even imagine the possibility of taking time out of a busy day to shut down, reload, and truly feel the exhilaration or peace of being worry free. Yet a few moments of positive energy should not be too much to ask. Even taking a moment to look up and notice the beauty in the sky that is there for us every day can help.

Make a conscious effort to slow the body down and give the brain some time to catch up. When your mind is at ease, your body will follow and you will relax; but if your body is in continual motion, your brain never has time to catch its breath. The mind can't come up with solutions to your problems, dream about the future, or even enjoy a moment of peaceful tranquility because your body is not giving it the time it needs to do its job. So block out even some small space on your calendar and add a few moments of good times to your hectic life. Then wear your white hat by keeping your promise and make sure you keep those sacred moments you put on your schedule, no matter what! Don't give in. Whatever happens in your day, make the time you scheduled for yourself precious. "No exceptions" are worth a few moments of your own time!

But all too soon time is up, playtime is over, and it's back to work. The good news is that once you become aware of just how much power time, money, stress and worry hold in your life, then hopefully you will be able to shift your thinking and adjust your priorities. Once you see the value in something it becomes easier to readjust your schedule so those new items get the required attention they deserve. Once again, things that are important to you must be moved higher up on your list of priorities. Readjusting your schedule, even just a small bit to include some quality time for yourself or time to focus on your family and friends, will bring significant changes to your long term vision.

If you are not playing the game of life with confidence, fun and passion, then you are at a disadvantage. All it takes is a small shift in your thinking and changes will appear. Remember that

A White Hat & Rose Colored Glasses

once we start looking for the things we desire they will begin to appear. We can't do that if we are too busy to even turn our heads and look around. So I urge you to re-evaluate your priorities and resources and make sure at least some of your precious time is allocated to the fun activities you want to attract more of. Give your brain the rest it is begging for. Your return on investment will be vast.

White Hat Awareness
BLOCK OUT SOME SPACE ON YOUR CALENDAR AND INCLUDE SOME GOOD TIMES TO YOUR HECTIC SCHEDULE

We are too busy being busy

Since we are talking about our priorities why is it that we work five days a week so we can enjoy two days off? Shouldn't it be the other way around? Probably, but for most people that is not the way their life works. All I can say is that if you only get two days a week off, you had better make sure there is some room in your weekends for the good stuff. Life simply cannot be all about work. Even in the old days when life was physically hard and you had to grow your own food and chop your own wood, they still set aside one day, usually Sunday for a day of rest.

How many times have we approached a friend or co-worker and can't even have a two minute conversation because they don't have the time. Sometimes people use being busy as an excuse to avoid things they don't really want to do. It is easier to say "I'm busy" then it is to say, "I'm not interested." And saying no can be uncomfortable so again, it's easier to say "I'm busy."

Nowadays people even choose to work on the weekends! Doesn't it seem strange that someone would choose to work instead of enjoying the little allotted time they have to enjoy their life? Yet it happens all the time. One reason could be that people like the safety of a routine. When life gets hectic and full of worries our learned response is to keep doing what we are doing only faster.

Soon being busy becomes a way of life, and this is dangerous because being busy can also send the message that we don't care. If someone doesn't have time for you, they may feel that they are not important in your life. We are often not even aware of this because we are too busy to notice. Our priorities have changed so that we like the feeling of getting things done and hopefully making more money for our efforts. It can almost become an addiction where we feel strange when we don't have a full list of things to do and places to be. Being busy is not necessarily a good thing. Plus we all know that when something is important to us, we can always find the time, and the money for the things we put at the top of our priority list. The things we value are the things we get done.

Another reason some people spend so much time working is because that is where they are comfortable. In order to go out and have a good time you have to work at it. Fun requires both physical and mental energy, so sometimes it is easier to go to work and turn on the autopilot. All you have to do is get into your routine and keep moving. Going out and having fun means you would have to socialize and engage with your surroundings. Plus you have to take the time to make yourself look good. You will have to think of interesting things to say and idle conversation is tiresome. Oh to heck with it! It's less trouble to go to work, and besides, I could use the extra money to buy more stuff.

With all of our technologies and innovative new time saving products, how is it that we now seem to be working harder with longer hours and less time off. If you ask me it looks like somewhere along the line our priorities changed. We have shifted our

A White Hat & Rose Colored Glasses

values towards a life of activity instead of a life that values people. I realize this is not a comforting idea, but maybe you need to put on your white hat and reevaluate your priorities and actions?

There is this story, one that has been told in many forms, about a fisherman sitting on the beach enjoying his life. He would fish just long enough to be able to make enough money for the basics. Then one day a businessman sat next to the man and asked him why he didn't buy a big boat. The fisherman asked why he needed one and the businessman suggested that he could then hire people to catch more fish. Again the fisherman asked why and the businessman responded that it would make him lots of money. Once again the fisherman pretended not to understand so the businessman tried to explain one last time. You need to make lots of money so you can retire and do nothing but sit on the beach all day long and fish – which is exactly what the fisherman was doing before the businessman came along.

White Hat Awareness
BEING BUSY IS DANGEROUS BECAUSE IT CAN SEND THE MESSAGE THAT WE DON'T CARE

Passion became a priority and everything changed

It's time for another story with a valuable lesson attached. When I was in college, I worked at a print shop. I was the kid behind the counter making copies. To speed up the story, years later the owner retired and I became owner of the business. Wow I even had employees and everything! Yet even though I had the benefits and pressures of owning a business, I still saw myself as that little girl behind the counter making copies. I acted more like an employee in my own company instead of the successful and confident business person I imagined. I was aware that I had to step up and embrace my role as business owner, but how?

Like I have said a million times, once you have awareness, your actions will follow and this was no exception. One day I had a flash of brilliance! I was going to take up golf because that is what business owners do. So I followed up on that inspiration and took decisive action by signing up for five golf lessons. As it turned out I love the game and it's become one of my passions.

Soon I was asked to play in a charity golf tournament. My automatic reaction was that it was too expensive and I couldn't possibly take a day off to play golf! Hey, wait a minute that is what the little girl behind the counter would say. A business person would say, "Heck yes!" From that mindset, the tournament was fun and I did some networking. I was one step closer to feeling like a true business owner. I also discovered that non-profit organizations did a lot of printing plus they are willing to trade printing for golf tournament fees. A win-win all around.

However I was still not quite there yet. I had my priorities in order because it was important to becoming the best entrepreneur I could be while still maintaining a balanced life, but for some reason I continued to see myself as the little girl behind the counter. This really sucked because I was a business owner. I wanted the business to grow and do great things but I knew that until I took ownership of my position I would continue to struggle. And then the opportunity presented itself and all I had to do was have the courage to take another action.

An old friend had an open spot in her weekly foursome and wanted me to join her. They teed off early in the morning so I could be done and back in the office by the afternoon. What? Commit to golfing once a week? No I can't do that. I'm too busy. Actually I am the boss now so technically I could take a morning off to golf if I wanted to. But no, I should be working not golfing. Hey wait a minute, aren't my priorities to become a business owner

A White Hat & Rose Colored Glasses

and have balance in my life? And wouldn't a weekly game of golf be in alignment with those priorities? So crazy as it seemed to me at the time, I said yes.

Once I committed to join them I became the entrepreneur I knew I could be. It was one of the best decisions I ever made. I chose to schedule one morning a week for golf. I made the time for something I was passionate about and I cannot fully explain the difference it made in my life. No matter how hectic my week is, as long as I have one morning to enjoy the time away, I can handle anything else the world throws my way.

And you know, committing to time for myself helped me make the mental shift I was looking for because business owners take mornings off to play golf - little girls behind the counter do not. I still don't understand why playing golf is acceptable in the business world. If I had told people that I was taking the morning off to go bowling or ride a bike, they would think I was crazy, maybe even irresponsible. But a morning off to play a round of golf is what business owners do, so that is what I do too. My priorities, passion, awareness, and actions changed everything.

White Hat Awareness
Get your priorities right and your life will start to change

White Hat Awareness for changing your Priorities

- Whatever you make a priority is what your mind will seek out

- Replace the squeaky wheel instead of greasing it

- If it's important – make it a priority

- Let positive emotions linger. They need more time to grow

- Commit to adding some good times to your hectic schedule

- Being busy can send the message that we don't care

- Get your priorities right and your life will start to change

Chapter 11

Courage:
Stand up for your beliefs

Becoming a hero in our own life means becoming aware, taking action, and doing what needs to be done. That means facing some rather uncomfortable feelings and having the courage to do it anyway. It is time to wear the white hat by keeping your promises, facing your fears, and being true to yourself. Begin your journey and own the life that you were meant to live.

Being the hero in your own life requires courage, but not the kind of courage where you are willing to risk your life or sacrifice everything to make someone else's life better. No the courage I'm talking about is more personal. It's about finding strength to take a stand, to fight for what you believe in. Have the guts to stand up for yourself and don't let others push you around. This self-centered kind of courage should not be thought of as selfish; rather, it should empower you to make those difficult decisions that will keep your priorities straight and your dreams alive.

Eye drops for your brain

The very fact that I am starting this section with the following story took a lot of courage on my part. What I am about to share

A White Hat & Rose Colored Glasses

is a rather personal story so I am facing the risk of judgment. The topic can be controversial, and is not filled with my typical happiness and joy, so a fear of rejection is something I must accept. However, I feel very strongly about including this material. I only hope that people will understand this is my personal quest and that I want them to be inspired to take a personal stand of their own. Standing up for what you truly believe takes courage and that is what this section is all about. So please keep an open mind as I share a story that you may totally disagree with.

I don't think most people fully comprehend the enormous influence the eye has on the brain. Once your brain gets a hold of an image it takes that single frame and blasts it into a hundred different directions. Understanding this is one of those eye-opening moments that will hang around in your head for a long time. It all became clear to me years ago after a group of us went to a sneak preview of the movie *Cliff Hanger*. Someone was talking about the movie and asked how I liked it. I said I wasn't a big fan because the movie was too violent for me.

My friends looked at me like I was crazy. It wasn't violent they said! Then I looked at them like they were crazy. You have to be kidding! They impaled someone on an ice spike, a guy was shot multiple times while trapped under the ice, and a man's face was ground into the dirt! I was astounded because all of those violent images were permanently implanted in the minds of my friends and they never gave it a second thought. Has our society really become that desensitized to violent acts? Apparently so.

This was a life changing insight for me. I don't like violent movies, but that *Cliff Hanger* incident made me aware of just how damaging those images can be. I personally believe that violent images are not good for society as a whole. Our brain is this super powerful computer that when you put any kind of data in, good or bad, the mind will spin that image into an endless number of other scenarios.

Susan Sherbert

Gee I never thought to kill a person with a straw but since you showed me how, now my brain can come up with twenty other ways to do damage with a straw. Multiply every horrendous footage of film, violent video game, or any negative image in your memory banks and the compound results the brain can extrapolate are frightening.

It was at that moment that I knew I had to do something, but what? I can't fight Hollywood and the amount of money made on violent video games is staggering. People already think I live in Fantasyland because of my rose colored glasses so what chance do I have to convince them to give up violent movies? None. However I also wear a white hat. That means I had to take action and do something. I did the only thing I knew how to do. I took responsibility for my own action and made an unwavering commitment to myself.

I decided that from that moment on I will no longer contribute to the problem. I will not allow my money to go towards violent movies, and I will not give my brain access to those awful images that I believe are harmful to society. People can argue, disagree, and tell me that I am totally wrong. I'm okay with that. I am not trying to change other people. They are free to watch all the violence they want.

This is about doing what I think is right. About standing up for what I believe in! From that day forward, the people and companies that make violent movies have not received one cent from me. I have had to turn down movie outings with my friends and I've been left out of certain conversations about popular films, but my position is important to me and my friends understand that.

Contrary to what you may think, I am not totally out of touch with reality. I like murder mysteries, crime, and suspense films and I understand that violence is part of life. Death and inhumanity are part of the story and I accept that. The difference is that now I have very clear criteria for what is acceptable for me

A White Hat & Rose Colored Glasses

and what is not. Knowing that makes it easier for me to hold that line, refuse to give in, and to honor the pledge I made to myself.

Another point I want to add is to share my theory as to how I think this whole violent image stuff got totally out of hand. It is my opinion the line was crossed with the movie Pulp Fiction. Now I admit I have never seen the move, and I'm glad my brain is not carrying around those terrible images, but to me there is something very wrong when the hero of a move is a hit man. When did it become okay to root for the bad guy! When did people start cheering when good guys and innocents get killed!

Why do you think I have a white hat in the title of this book? Because good guys wear white and you should want the good guy to win. You want them to be the hero. Before that movie people knew who they were cheering for. The hero at least tried to do the right thing. Now the whole good guy/bad guy line is so mixed up who knows what to think anymore. Just kill them all and the one left standing must be the hero. Who wants to live in a society like that? Not me. I want to be the hero and wear the white hat. I want to know who the good guys and bad guys are.

Again, I do not expect you to give up violent movies or violent video games, however I do hope that this story brings awareness to just how many potentially damaging images are being implanted in your brain every day. Simply bringing awareness to what you are watching is all I ask. Remember, one image can easily turn into a hundred other ideas. Start to pay attention to the images you are feeding your brain. Put the good stuff in so you can get even better stuff out. And parents, what images are you allowing to be planted in the very fertile minds of your children!

White Hat Awareness
PUT THE GOOD STUFF IN SO YOU CAN GET EVEN BETTER STUFF OUT

Susan Sherbert

I couldn't let it go

I made my non-violent commitment years ago but recently, I was presented with a test of my commitment. I saw an image on a website of Santa in a military plane holding a big gun with the caption "Santa cleaning up his naughty list." Now I can totally understand how this is could be seen as funny, however the image that went from my eye to my brain was not amusing to me because I had taken a stand against violence. The site was supposed to be clean and funny and this particular image totally crossed my personal line. It was something that I just couldn't let go.

I responded back about how in my opinion the picture was not funny and that Santa is a childhood hero so he shouldn't be made into a killer. I realize you may think I'm overreacting but remember *I am fully aware that images we see stay in our heads for the rest of our lives. We can never delete them.*

I was also fully aware that one comment in social media could go terribly wrong very quickly. Sure enough there was a rapid response from the person who posted the image saying that he was a military man and that our troops needed protecting etc. I could not disagree with him so I was very careful in my response. I replied that we all have differences of opinions and that we were having a good discussion. I agree that our troops need to be protected, but also pointed out that because of my strong beliefs against casual violent images in society I would not have been true to myself if I did not comment about that picture. Both sides had made their points and we agreed to disagree. In the end I was glad I spoke up because this is my personal mission. I never want to pick a fight or add more negativity and hostility to a situation, however I must respectfully stand up for what I feel strongly about - it's a white hat thing.

A White Hat & Rose Colored Glasses

White Hat Awareness
Make a commitment to yourself

Courage to do nothing

A phrase I really like is about not confusing kindness with weakness. Just because someone is nice and pleasant instead of harsh and aggressive does not make them weak. In fact I believe there is tremendous value in the power of knowing when to do nothing. Turn the other cheek is a good example. If someone is aggressive and attacking you, it seems only natural to want to defend yourself and do damage in return, to make the offender pay. Have the courage to stand up and fight back! The last story proves that I agree with standing up for what you believe in, however I don't always agree with the methods people use. It takes a strong person, a true good guy hero to walk way.

Martin Luther King, Gandhi, and Nelson Mandela are all examples of the courage it takes to do nothing. Gee doesn't that sound funny? These courageous men did nothing and ended up making history. They didn't return the anger they were confronted with. They didn't seek revenge. They were firm and did not engage. They were kind but never ever weak. This is one of those big awareness moments because sometimes one of the most courageous acts you could ever do is have the strength to do nothing.

If that insight has you motivated to go out and do nothing let me attach a little warning notice to the inside of your white hat. It would say "Warning: to delay is to decide." Doing nothing can be a weakness or a strength. It is not courageous to avoid difficult choices, run away from your problems, or bury your head in the sand. Making no decision is not the same thing as deciding to do nothing. If you choose to avoid something that means you are giving the opportunity permission to pass, or hoping the problem will go way. Not making a decision leads to inaction and that is a poor choice. It's the decisions behind the action that determine the impact of doing nothing.

White Hat Awareness
MARTIN LUTHER KING, GANDHI, AND NELSON MANDELA ARE ALL EXAMPLES OF THE COURAGE IT TAKES TO DO NOTHING

Sorry, I apologize for the confusion

I never know where my brain is going to take me as I begin to write, and this next section took some very strange turns. I knew I wanted to include a white hat awareness step about having the courage to apologize but I certainly never knew that "I'm sorry" would be mixed into the equation. This is one of those times when I know that humans are crazy - totally mixed up, get it all backwards, make no sense, and kind of crazy.

It all started when I saw a blurb that mentioned that people say "I'm sorry" something like twelve times a day. That got my attention. My original plan was to write about how difficult it is for people to apologize and admit that they are wrong. You know, politicians lie and cover up instead of facing the obvious mistake with courage and simply acknowledging that they were wrong. Or how about spouses when they know they messed up and forgot an anniversary or birthday? Instead of admitting they are wrong, people too often justify, point fingers, and make excuses. It has to be anyone else's fault but their own. Time to get a lawyer and sue someone... but I digress.

A White Hat & Rose Colored Glasses

Admitting mistakes and accepting responsibility for your choices or bad behavior shouldn't be so hard. We are humans we mess up. We miscalculate, give in to temptations, and do things we are not proud of. If we can learn from our mistakes and honestly tell others that we meant no harm then we can reduce the guilt and anger and let the hurt feelings begin to heal. It should be that simple, but it is not.

Back to the crazy. How can it possibly be that we can't apologize to the people we love dearly yet we can say "I'm sorry" multiple times a day? We profusely apologize because we did nothing more than step in the path of a total stranger. We easily say "I'm sorry the place is untidy" or "Sorry I missed your call" but we can't apologize to our own parents for not including them in the plans for a second wedding. Even if we just touched a stranger's shoulder and it was actually their fault because they bumped into us, we still accept full responsibility and apologize with "I'm sorry."

How can that be? It makes no logical sense. Fights happen, marriages are lost, politicians are mocked all because people refuse to apologize and take responsibility for their mistakes. So why in the world do we apologize to strangers and acquaintances twelve times a day? We apologize and say "I'm sorry" for everything and anything that is insignificant in our lives, yet we get stubborn and dig in our heels when it is truly important to make amends for our poor judgment. Can anyone explain that one to me? Crazy I say. Simply crazy.

I'm not even sure how to summarize this section. Shouldn't there be some clear rules of wisdom or good advice I can offer? I suppose all I can really say is stop being so stubborn and apologize when you hurt people you care about; and stop being so ridiculous and quit saying "I'm sorry" to strangers when you didn't do anything wrong. I realize I went a little crazy myself on this whole apology lesson so please forgive me. Sorry but I just had to rant.

Susan Sherbert

White Hat Awareness
STOP SAYING YOU ARE SORRY AND APOLOGIZE FOR YOUR MISTAKES

You are an adult now

You are an adult now. Don't forget that. What that means is that you don't need your parents' permission or approval. You get to choose what movies to watch, what friends to have and what route you take to work. You can stay up late, eat junk food, and play loud music if you desire. If you have a partner or spouse, they certainly have influence in your life, but in the end you are responsible for your own actions. You make your own decisions and you give yourself permission to accept or reject just about everything you do.

Sure you can seek the advice of others and value their opinions, but you must be true to yourself and have the guts to stand firm, disagree, and let your thoughts be known. Yet too often we feel the need to have other people's consent or approval before we take action. To wear the white hat you need to find the courage to give yourself the authority to do what needs to be done. The permission is granted by you.

I see permission connected to power. When you feel the need to ask someone else if it's okay to do something then you are assuming they have the power or authority to give their consent. It can be something as simple as, "Can I buy some girl scout cookies from the neighbor?" or "Can I go out for a drink after work?" My question is do you really need to ask someone else's permission for small things like that? Again, you are an adult now so take the responsibility for your own decisions and stop letting others make decisions for you.

A White Hat & Rose Colored Glasses

I realize that life can be complicated and there is a balance between being polite and being rude. It is only good manners to be respectful of other people by asking their permission to borrow their stuff, use their things or even pet their dog. And of course you wouldn't plan an event or go out of town without asking your spouse, roommate or friend if it interferes with something they had already planned. But if you want to catch up with an old friend or even buy a new pair of socks, you shouldn't have to have permission. A big part of being a grown-up is acknowledging that you have the power to make your own decisions, so stop giving that power away.

White Hat Awareness
The permission is granted by you

"I want" should be included in your vocabulary

You may or may not have a big cause or issue that you feel strongly about like my whole anti-violence thing, however I am pretty sure there are tons of small areas that would enhance your life if you only decided to hold your ground and stand up for what you wanted. If you have forgotten to include yourself on the list of people you make happy, the solution is quite simple. Start by allowing very small wants back into your life. Make decisions that benefit you! In order to wear that white hat and be more courageous you must learn to stand up for things that are important to you. It doesn't have to be a big social issue. The small stuff should count too.

For example one night I got home late and decided I wanted a bowl of cereal for dinner. Unfortunately the milk was bad. Oh well, what I wanted didn't really matter, so I started to look for something else to eat. Then I stopped and thought, no I really want a bowl of cereal. Am I not even worth a five minute trip to the store to get milk?

If a family member had said they felt like ice cream I wouldn't hesitate to go out and get them some. But if it is something I want it's too much trouble? Now that is just plain wrong. I deserve better. So guess what? I went out, got some milk, and enjoyed my bowl of cereal, and boy did it taste good.

As a little kid, life is all about desires and happiness. "I want" is part of their daily life. Kids see something they want and they think it should be theirs. Life is all about what makes them happy. Then life changes and we grow-up. Somehow our days are now spent trying to give everyone else what they want so they can be happy. We try to make our kids happy so if that means a soccer game instead to a facial, that is what we do. If we were planning on a quiet night at home but our friends want to come over to watch the game, we give in because they are our friends.

All of these kinds of decisions are to please other people, but what about what you want? What about your happiness? Maybe you have let it go so far that you don't even know what you want anymore. Are you so grown-up that wishes and yearnings for happy things are no longer allowed in your thoughts?

If the words "I want" are no longer in your grown-up vocabulary then things need to change. We need to learn to love ourselves again. Of course we can't really go back to the spoiled brat stage and demand to have everything we like, but we shouldn't totally suppress our feelings for things that bring us joy either.

The key to so many things in life is balance. Kids want it all but need to learn that sometimes you don't get everything you want. Some grown-ups want nothing but need to learn that sometimes you do need to get what you want. So if you want an ice cream or a bowl of cereal for dinner, have the dang ice cream or enjoy breakfast for dinner. Learn to let "I want" become a part

A White Hat & Rose Colored Glasses

of your balanced way of life. If something brings you even small moments of joy then by all means have it! Small changes like remembering to think of yourself are a wonderful way to start bringing the good things back into your life.

White Hat Awareness
What you want, matters

1. Love yourself. Love others
2. Forgive yourself. Forgive others
3. Respect yourself. Respect others
4. Listen to yourself. Listen to others
5. Take care of yourself. Take care of others

Green cape and purple boots

Keeping with the "I want" theme, remember when we were kids and had the freedom to think without limits? If we wanted to wear a green cape and purple boots to school we put on the outfit and got ready for the day. What other people thought didn't even enter our little brains because we were carefree. We didn't understand judgment, peer pressure, or even the need to get along. Heck we were only just learning how to share.

Then enter the parents. Now these guys fully understand all of the grown-up "rules" so they won't allow us to wear our favorite outfit to school. Maybe you screamed and yelled and got your way, or maybe you knew your parents wouldn't give in so you didn't push back. Either way, it was the beginning of the awareness that you are part of society and not everyone agrees with you. Sometimes you have to give in or compromise to fit in and get along.

Since then we have been taught the importance of working together. We've learned to be conscious of the needs and desires of others and we understand that our wants are not always practical. We realize that other people have feelings and that our actions have an impact on others. Like it or not, our actions, opinions, and desires are now influenced by what other people might think.

Okay some people don't care as much as others so they have the courage to wear what they want, and do crazy and unusual things - but most of us are not that brave. We don't skip in public, carry around our teddy bears, or wear a green cape and purple boots to work. We want to fit in, be accepted, and please others. Other people now influence our lives and we want to be a part of their world. We are no longer that carefree child who lives in a world of their own. When getting dressed for work we pass up our purple cowboy boots and dress to impress.

Even simple everyday occurrences are not immune from our desire to please others. Let's say someone asks you what you want to eat. You feel like pizza, but you don't want to be thought of as unhealthy or you don't want to come across as bossy or controlling, so you shrug your shoulders, fib and say you don't care. Someone suggests a sandwich, so you join the crowd and have a sandwich for lunch. Heck you didn't really want pizza. A sandwich sounds tasty.

How stupid is all of that? You didn't even suggest the possibility of having pizza plus you added a little white cover up lie so you wouldn't disagree with someone or upset their feelings. Again, why? There was no necessity to try to please your friends in that circumstance. What, would your friends think less of you because you want pizza for lunch? And if you did happen to stand up for yourself and actually tell the truth about wanting pizza, would you then feel the need to justify your truth by explaining

A White Hat & Rose Colored Glasses

that you had an extra-long workout that morning so you could afford the calories?

Just because you prefer something different doesn't make you bad, wrong, or even an outcast. We think that if we agree with people they will like us. The reality is trying to please people only helps us blend in and go unnoticed. Being honest and being ourselves is what will make us popular with the right kind of people - the people who like us and accept us for who we are.

Trying to belong doesn't mean we have to be the same. Uniqueness is important because we are all different. Some of us are the hare that likes to run fast. Others are the tortoise, preferring to plod along at their own pace. As we move through life, fast or slow, it is important to remember that we are all humans in this race called life. We want to fit in and be loved, yet we should also want to be recognized for our own unique contributions as well.

What other people think about you does matter, at least to some degree, so my suggestion is that instead of trying so hard to fit in and be part of the crowd, why not embrace what makes you different? If you become your own person and voice your opinions, you will begin to stand out. Not in the green cape in purple boots kind of way. Instead you will stand out because you had the courage to have an open and honest opinion. People will admire you more for being true to who you are instead of just going along with the crowd. You gain trust and respect by standing out with your actions and that just may help you become one of the leaders in the group you are trying so hard to please.

White Hat Awareness
Don't try to fit in by pleasing everyone, gain their respect by standing out

Susan Sherbert

Silence is unheard of

They say that silence is golden and I can think of many times when that is oh so true. Yet silence can also feel really awkward. You know what I mean. You are having a conversation with people you just met and suddenly there is that uncomfortable silence filled with tension. Quick! Fill the void and say something about the weather to keep that conversation going.

It is so strange and I have no idea how silence can be that uncomfortable, but when it happens the silence is downright scary. On the other hand, when you are with people you are comfortable with you can sit with them in silence for hours. No conversation required. Life is funny that way.

Since life is all about balance and awareness I would like to point out that way too often we simply talk too much. We talk, talk, talk and forget to listen. We feel the need to explain every detail and include all the facts. It seems that as long as we keep talking the person will be required to give us attention. But that is so not true. It's the opposite in fact. The less we talk, the more concise we are, the more powerful are words become.

Yet we continue to talk and people continue to pretend to listen. When people talk too much our minds switch off and we think about something else. We are no longer listening. The words have no meaning. Yet we nod, and occasionally mumble something just to be polite. The message was lost after the third sentence but the words keep coming. It is no longer a conversation.

The white hat lesson many of us need to work on is the power to be quiet and listen. Have the courage to stop talking and give the other person your full attention. Allow silence into a conversation. Wait just one tiny moment before you speak. Give yourself time to think of a clear and concise response. This is where the "less is more" phrase is a valuable lesson.

A White Hat & Rose Colored Glasses

A perfect example - I recently went around and asked my friends to give me one word to describe themselves. I gave them plenty of silence and space so they could come up with their own answer and I was very pleased with the results. In fact I was amazed even, because in just one word, most people were able to give me a very clear and accurate description of themselves - in just one word. Someone was kind, another was nurturing. Compulsive, analytical, patient, and passionate were also used. And when I asked one friend she said friendly. That is not the word I might have chosen but the truth is, friendly fit my friend better than anything I could have come up with.

So back to the point. Sometimes all that is required is a simple response, not long detailed explanations filled with insignificant details. Why use ten words when the clarity of one word - the right word - leaves no room for doubt? Have the courage to keep it short and simple and then wait for a response. Resist the temptation to talk. Accept the silence. The goal should be clarity and that means less information, not more. Fill the silence with your focus and attention instead of more words.

White Hat Awareness
Have the courage to allow silence into a conversation — it's called listening

White Hat Awareness for Courage

- Put the good stuff in so you can get even better stuff out
- Make a commitment to yourself
- It takes true courage to do nothing
- Stop saying you are sorry and apologize for your mistakes
- The permission is granted by you
- What you want, matters
- Don't try to fit in, gain respect by standing out
- Allow silence into a conversation – it's called listening

Chapter 12

Gratitude:
Appreciate everything

There are so many positive things in life that we could be thankful for but we spend far too much time and energy focusing on negativity. Like I have said many times before, our brains are programmed to see the bad stuff first. That is just how it is. This chapter is about gratitude so if we want to take action and do the things we need to do, it is time to start looking for the good stuff. It all around us. We just need to remember to look for the positive energy and bring gratitude and appreciation to our attention.

Receive the gifts you are being are offered

You hear about people doing random acts of kindness all the time. Well one day that kindness was bestowed on me and I have to tell you it felt pretty darn good!

I had family visiting so we went out to our favorite place to eat. The restaurant was busy and we were given a table for two kind of squashed between two other tables. We hardly noticed the other diners because we had a lot of catching up to do. Drinks were ordered and our favorite meals were served. Then towards the end of our meal the people to our right stood up, leaned over and said, "My daughter and I like to do something kind for other people so we have paid for your meal."

What! This doesn't happen in real life!

We looked at each other almost in shock as the random act of kindness people tried to quietly make their exit. I didn't know what to do so I jumped up and gave each of them a big hug. We spoke for all of thirty seconds and then these generous people headed out the door. Random act of kindness successfully delivered.

That one simple act of paying for a meal left the two of us on cloud nine for hours. Days even. Those two strangers were just being nice and I'm assuming they did it because they wanted to share their generosity with others. Family and friends do kind things for each other all the time so why did their random act of kindness have such a powerful impact on me? Somehow a show of caring from a total stranger seemed to amplify the meaning of their gift.

What I discovered was that when generosity is received from a total stranger that gift is one hundred percent pure. There are no strings attached, no expectations, and no need to reciprocate. Their kindness was given, and received freely, and that just doesn't happen often enough in society today. We have learned to become skeptical when we accept something from others because we think there may be a catch. We give gifts because we feel obligated to do so or we may even question the intentions behind a simple compliment.

When our thoughts become focused on what we must give in return, we forget to appreciate the thoughtfulness and devalue the kindness being was offered. But think about it. Most people don't give gifts, or do kind things, because they want something in return. They offer presents to show their appreciation and let you know that you matter.

Maybe it's time to bring back your childhood schooling and

remember that it truly is the thought that counts. See the gratitude in the gift and don't feel bad about receiving kindness from other people. Accept the present, compliment, or assistance without the guilt. Welcome, receive, and appreciate the generosity they choose to give.

White Hat Awareness
GIVE AND RECEIVE KINDNESS FREELY WITH NO CONDITIONS OR EXPECTATIONS

The simple act of Thank You

Taking this kindness even further, try to remember that people like to help. Giving and sharing what we have is a pleasure. We are not imposing on someone when they offer assistance. They are offering us a part of themselves because it feels good for both sides. Giving and receiving are a positive part to life. So why is it so hard to openly accept the help or nice gesture that is being offered? Why do people resist something as simple as a little bit of kindness?

When someone offers to help you - let them! It may be something as simple as an offer to carry your bag, to share an umbrella, or to hold your drink. It is their gift to you so accept the assistance and be grateful. Because you are a grown-up now you wouldn't want to take advantage of people and you probably don't actually need the help, but why refuse an offer that was made in kindness? Accept their help and be glad of the assistance.

If someone offers you something the chances are it is because they like you and it is their way of showing you that they care. Then why do we have to say things like, "Oh you shouldn't have" or "Thanks, but that wasn't necessary." Of course it wasn't necessary.

A White Hat & Rose Colored Glasses

Most of the time people do nice things because they want to, not because they have to. And someone once pointed out that people will go to the end of the Earth for nothing more than a smile. A small but powerful symbol that sends the message that their generosity has meaning.

Embrace thoughtful gestures and let the pleasures of good deeds linger. Try to give openly with no expectations and remember to receive generosity the same way. Welcome positive energy in and give it some of the space that is reserved for the negativity we subconsciously focus on every day.

The White Hat lesson I am trying to convey is to simply appreciate the gifts you are being offered. Receive kindness with a warm and genuine thank you. Honest appreciation should be all that is required. A true show of gratitude is a gift in itself. The next time someone offers to buy you coffee, dinner, or pitch in for gas don't fight over it. Look the person straight in the eye and say a heartfelt thank you. Don't discount their generosity with resistance, and certainly don't feel guilty about "taking" the kindness. They want to give so don't reject their kindness! Smile and let them know you truly appreciate what they are offering.

White Hat Awareness
Let a heartfelt thank you be enough

Oh it was nothing

Next we need to show gratitude and appreciation to ourselves. Far too often we can't even freely accept something as simple as a compliment! How many times do people deflect kind words with phrases like, "Oh it was nothing" or "It was no trouble." When someone tells you that they like something you have or that you did a good job, don't explain it away like it was nothing. Your effort and input counts and you are worthy of receiving the appreciation. Don't discount your actions. Value and acknowledge the gratitude. Compliments and praise are given with positive intentions so they should be received with positive acceptance in return.

It makes no sense why people belittle their actions by describing all of the flaws, but we hear it all the time. "I really like the new décor." "Thanks but we did it on a budget and it's not the exact color we wanted." What! Was that negative response really necessary! Yet those "Thanks, but..." kind of responses are far too common. "Thanks, but it wasn't my idea." "Thanks, but it was really no big deal." My challenge to you is to get off your butt and stop adding but's where they don't belong. Learn to respond with a simple thank you from the heart instead! Nothing more is required.

White Hat Awareness
ELIMINATE "THANKS, BUT..." FROM YOUR VOCABULARY

Nice Shirt

This is the opposite side of the oh it was nothing - This is the story about how showing untruthful appreciation can do more harm than good. I had one friend who loved to give compliments. "Nice shirt!" she would say. She would always give you some type of positive comment every time she saw you. People love compliments and her words did make me feel pretty good. Yet after a while, I became skeptical. She had become like the little boy who cried wolf by continually offering false and insincere praise. I began to wonder if she was being genuine with her compliments.

A White Hat & Rose Colored Glasses

Every single time I saw her, she would compliment my clothes. I remember one time I was wearing a basic T-shirt, and I think there was even a hole in it, yet I still received the "nice shirt" compliment. It felt like I could walk in wearing dirty old painting clothes and she would still say nice shirt. Eventually I began to doubt her sincerity and mistrust began to slowly creep in.

Of course complimenting people is a positive thing, but it must be done with sincerity. A compliment should be truthful or it's like those "how you doing" lies where all the small tiny unconscious lies build up and turn into distrust. When compliments are insincere people feel it and the power of their kindness is diminished. Without meaning behind the statement, compliments are simply empty words.

White Hat Awareness
Don't say it if you are not sincere

Criticism shouldn't be fun

Gratitude and appreciation are habits we should cultivate. Criticism and judgment are habits we should avoid. Yet it is hard because we go back to the fact that our brain is simply trying to protect us by focusing on the negative. We see negativity and flaws first so it kind of makes sense that we find fault and pick on people. "Did you see how awful John looked yesterday?" "Look at that terrible outfit. What was she thinking" "I heard that Sally had been drinking" Etc. Etc. It's like when we have a bad experience at a store or in a restaurant. We go out and tell everybody about the rude waiter or stupid employee and we remember the negative story for years and years. Yet when people do good things we don't repeat their stories too often.

Susan Sherbert

We don't mean to gossip and make fun of people yet we do it in an almost subconscious manner. Don't let criticism become your way of life. Have the guts to stand up and stop conversations that pick on people, make fun of their mistakes, or are simply not nice. It takes both a talker and a listener to have a conversion so even if you don't start the criticism you shouldn't support it by listening to it either. Wear your white hat and say no thanks I'm not listening to gossip, let's find something nice to say about the person instead.

White Hat Awareness
Instead of participating in gossip, find something positive to say about the person instead

Our most under used asset

I know I wear rose colored glasses, but to me a smile is one of the most powerful actions we can take. It hardly requires any effort at all yet that one tiny movement of our lips has magical powers. A smile can change our mood, convey messages words cannot, and it can even bring us to tears of both laughter and joy. Smiles are an unlimited supply, free to use, and they contain superpowers that can change the world. So why don't we take advantage of this incredible asset that we have had since birth? Heck if I know.

As kids we laughed, smiled and giggled all the time. As adults, not so much. For some unknown reason we simply forget to smile. And it's not like smiling takes a whole lot of effort. It's not painful like facing the truth. Smiles don't take up our valuable time. They don't require money or additional education to use. We don't have to uncover some limiting belief to realize smiles

A White Hat & Rose Colored Glasses

are a good thing. We can even share a smile with no obligation, commitments or expectations required. The only thing we have to do to tap into the incredible asset we already possess, is to remember to use it! So that is my advice to you. Simply remember to smile big every single day.

White Hat Awareness
Remember to smile every day

Almost forgot

It's so typical. How often do we forget to be grateful for and appreciate the people that love and support us the most? It's odd really because we do take our closest friends and family for granted. It's okay to vent on them when we are angry or hurt. They are there to support and love us so they understand our bad moods. Of course they don't mind taking up the slack when things get tough. They are there for us in good times and bad. All of that is true and that is what family and friends do. So yes it will happen - we will take our loved ones for granted.

This idea was stored in that silly subconscious part of my brain until one day I went into an office and there were flowers on the desk. I asked if it was a birthday or something and she said no, it was just because. And I thought, "Wow! Just because. What an awesome reason to give someone flowers!" Not because we are reminded to do so by a date on a calendar. Not because we feel bad or guilty and need to say I'm sorry. And not because the person is sad or needs cheering up. Giving flowers for no particular reason is probably the best reason of all. It shows our family and friends that we are grateful to have them in our lives and that we appreciate them every day, even on days when there is no specific reason.

White Hat Awareness

SHOW APPRECIATION TO THOSE CLOSEST TO YOU FOR NO PARTICULAR REASON

White Hat Awareness for Gratitude

- Give and receive freely with no conditions or expectations
- Let a heartfelt thank you be enough
- Eliminate "thanks, but..." from your vocabulary
- Don't say it if you are not sincere
- Avoid gossip, find something positive to say instead
- Remember to smile every day
- Show appreciation for no particular reason

Chapter 13
Determination:
Never give up

Keep trying. Never give up!

You are reading this because I never gave up. Being an author has been a dream of mine for years. In fact, I'm almost too embarrassed to mention that my first book, *Grown-ups Don't Skip*, took nearly twenty years to complete. It went through countless revisions and even more rejections. But I will never give up my dream. I admit I put my dream aside for a while and went away to pout. Yet somehow I always manage to come back around to keeping my vision alive.

It all started because I've always had the party house. Over the years I had gathered so much material on party games, icebreakers and creative entertaining that one day the spark hit and I thought, why not write a book! One of the reasons I give such good parties is because I always try to get everyone to participate. That included my adopted eighty year old grandma. She inspired the title of my first attempt at a book and *My Grandma Plays Twister* became a manuscript about party games for grown-ups.

REALITY CHECK NUMBER ONE: I did my research and learned all about query letters so I sent a batch to some publishers.

A White Hat & Rose Colored Glasses

Yippee! I found a publisher that was interested in my book. That's great, I'd be a bestseller by the end of the year… except the publisher asked for a book proposal. Book proposal? What in the heck is that? Little did I know that it would take me over three months to determine my target market, create an outline, write several sample chapters, and check off a few other requested items. Never give up, remember? It was an amazing process and I learned a lot, but I'm not sure exactly what happened. Life gets in the way of life so the book and the book proposal ended up on hold for a while.

"Keep on trying. Never give up on your dreams." Life continued on but my dream of helping people have more fun never quite went away. Then one day I found a writers' conference coming to my area so I figured, why not! It was expensive, but it was a writers' conference so with some professional advice, I'd be selling tons of books so money won't be a huge issue. Off I went with my book and proposal in my bag. Again, I found someone who liked the idea, but they suggested I change the title and then asked for my marketing plan! A what?

Reality Check Number Two: This never give up stuff was really starting to suck. The marketing plan was the part where my dream hit that wall of reality. Where childhood imagination met grown-up obstacles. This was also the part where you must keep believing that anything is possible. Yes it was difficult, yes it was hard work, and yes I had to keep my rose colored glasses in place. I don't know how I was going to finish a marketing plan. I had no idea how to develop a loyal following and attract readers, but as long as I kept one tiny little crack open, my dream would continue to live. My motivation continued to fade and life continued to tick away so once again, the book, and my dream, was put on hold. But you can be sure that I started to pay attention to things like blogs, websites, and social media.

What? My dream is still possible? I told you I would never give up. Technology and time are powerful things - and the internet was and is a really great teacher. The next wave of momentum came when someone just happened to mention a website that helps authors self-publish books on the internet. My friend was in a church book club and almost every single member has access to Kindle books so I needed to look into this digital publishing thing.

For whatever reason in addition to my big book I had been writing fun little corny joke books as well. I had a whole stack of them in the office just sitting there waiting to be discovered. Okay so corny jokes books were not the visions in my dream, but when opportunity knocks you have to answer the door. So to keep the dream alive, I turned my joke collection into silly eBooks I could use to test the market. Even with 52 corny joke books up on Amazon I was only making enough money to buy a cup of hot chocolate or maybe a doughnut or two.

That was okay because I knew life was a learning process; a test to see what I was made of. I had come this far and couldn't give up on my dream. I discovered all about internet marketing and so much more. My Halloween Corny joke book even hit number one in its category with over 4,000 downloads all over the world. Hey that makes me an Amazon Best Seller... but wait, I was only making about $20 a month. That was the reality part, but where in the heck was the dream part?

It took me another year and a half, and some major life changes but finally I finished my book about having more fun. Yippee! And I am happy to say that to this day I am still super proud of *Grown-ups Don't Skip Have FUN Be Happy Enjoy Life*. It's a real book with pages and everything. You can buy it on Amazon in paperback or digital. That means I am now living the dream!

REALITY CHECK ONE THOUSAND AND COUNTING: Just because a book is published doesn't mean people will rush out to buy it. You have to go out and market the darn thing! I guess that means I am back to the learning process, again. This time I decided to take everything I learned and start fresh with a second book. This book, *A White Hat and Rose Colored Glasses* is the result and I can honestly say it is so much better because of all of the rejections of the past. I have learned so much over the years that the ideas keep flowing and I have enough material left over for book number three.

Yet whatever happens next, I will not let that grown-up voice talk me out of moving my dreams forward! I will continue to proudly wear my rose colored glasses and I will continue to enjoy the journey wherever it takes me.

White Hat Awareness

Reality is hard because it never quite matches the stuff that you visualize

Chapter 14

Conclusion

If you are thinking a little bit differently from when you first picked up this book then I have done my job. My purpose was to bring clarity and awareness to your thoughts so you could do something about changing the habits that are not working in your life.

The first part of this book was all about changing your vision. Hopefully you have been inspired to put on your rose colored glasses and are seeing the things you need to see. You should now be aware of some of the limiting beliefs that are getting in your way. Awareness is a powerful force because we do so many things without thinking about them. Our unconscious thoughts produce tons of feelings that result in unwanted actions. We need to change that.

Our bodies only want to protect us so that means the first thing we focus on are the negative sides of almost everything. The positive thoughts and emotions are there, we just need to look a little harder to see them. Be aware of the dominance of negativity and begin to truly look for the good stuff. And that is where your rose colored glasses come in. Use them to shift your attention so you can see those light bulb moments, and discover the tiny seeds of possibility. Give your imagination the energy it needs to grow into the life of your dreams.

A White Hat & Rose Colored Glasses

> WEAR YOUR ROSE COLORED GLASSES SO YOU CAN SEE THE THINGS YOU NEED TO SEE!

That just about covers the rose colored glasses part of the book. Now on to the white hat. Once again it is all about awareness. Paying attention to your inner thoughts is the foundation for building your new and improved life. However it is only part of what will make your changes happen - the easy part. The good guy white hat is where the real work begins. The saying goes "This is what separates the boys from the men," but I'll change that to say this is what separates the successful from the ordinary.

I can feel people nodding their heads in agreement, until they read the next sentence. I'm about to tell you things you probably don't want to hear. If you want to be the hero in your own life and achieve the success you know is within you, then you must actually do something about it. We can think all we want, but to achieve any lasting results in life, we must put our new enlightened insights into action. Moving towards the life you desire requires that you take action; but it must be the right action. Have the courage to make the difficult decisions and chose the paths that point in the direction of your dreams.

> PUT ON THE GOOD GUY WHITE HAT AND DO THE THINGS YOU NEED TO DO!

Respect

Our white hat hero lessons wouldn't be complete if I didn't include some thoughts about respect. As I began to summarize the lessons I have shared in this book, I was very surprised that I had not included something about respect. What surprised me even more was that I could not find a single negative definition, or reference to the word respect, that was not full of positive attributes. Respect it appears is nothing but good!

When you have courage you earn the respect of others. When you keep your promises you gain respect. When you make hard choices and do the right things, you can hold your head high and have respect for yourself. But it goes even further. We should respect and honor our environment. We need to be more supportive and courteous to those less fortunate, and we need to be respectful and appreciative of the possessions we are privileged to own.

One memorable life lesson about respect came from a story I remember about Walt Disney. I don't remember the exact quote but his message basically said that if you hold something in high regard and appreciate its value, people will respect it. They will appreciate its worth and treat it with integrity and decency. However, and this is a big however, if you let that value drop, even a little bit people will run it into the ground and treat it with total disregard.

This is true for physical things but the philosophy also applies to people as well. For example, maybe you get a brand new bright and shiny car. You love and respect your new ride so you are careful with it. You admire and even treasure the flawless appearance and hold your car in high regard. You don't want to scratch it so you are very conscious of where you park. You are slow and deliberate when loading and unloading cargo from the trunk and if a friend wants to take it through a drive thru, no way! You sure as heck aren't going to allow people to eat or drink in your brand new car.

Now let's imagine this time the car is very clean and very nice but it is a used car. There may be a slight scratch or worn bit here and there. Overall the car is in pretty good shape. You are careful getting in and out of the car, and you are conscious of where you park but you don't make a huge issue about it. You are hungry

A White Hat & Rose Colored Glasses

one night after work and see a drive thru so what the heck, a few tiny crumbs won't hurt anything. Soon the car has lost some of its value plus it has lost some of your respect.

    Walt understood that if you respect something others will too. But, as I wrote before, if you let it go even one tiny bit, people will run it into the ground. Another great example is Disneyland itself. The place is clean, immaculate even. There isn't one piece of trash on the ground. I have seen parades with thousands of people and tons of confetti flying everywhere and within minutes the streets are clean and put back in proper order. The reason for this is because of respect. If there is no trash anywhere in sight, you don't want to be the first person to litter. You hold on to your trash until you find a proper place to put it. Of course they made sure there are plenty of trash cans available so you wouldn't be tempted to disrespect his kingdom.

    Now if there had already been a piece of trash on the ground, or even a wrapper up against the receptacle, you are likely to still make an effort to discard your trash. But if you missed the bin you could easily be tempted to leave your trash there adding to the pile. Like I just said, if you respect it people will too. If you let things go, the disrespect will spiral out of control. This is such a perfect example with so many things in life. Walt was a wise man indeed. I don't know if he actually wore a white hat, but I am pretty sure he owned a pair of rose colored glasses.

    Okay one more quick tribute to Walt. He said, "*All of our dreams can come true if we have the courage to pursue them.*" In other words, once you have the clarity of your dreams, you must take action and pursue them. Again, it's all about clarity and action!

Susan Sherbert

Shaking the snow globe

To conclude this adventure of ours let me leave you with one last story. I have this friend who refers to me as her snow globe. Why? Because I have been known to shake her beliefs with a jolt of awareness, and once those new thoughts start bouncing around in her head they are pretty hard to ignore. Awareness is a good thing but it can make your life feel unsettled and unclear. Luckily the emotions calm down and the uncomfortable feelings go away. Then your vision clears and you begin to see things a little bit differently. You are now more open and receptive to new ideas, and some of your limiting beliefs have shifted.

Shaking the snow globe is good because when you stir up awareness, it is the beginning of change. The way I see it is that it is better to face something that may make you feel uncomfortable, instead of trying to protect yourself, or others, with a lie. In the short term the truth is difficult to handle, but in the end the truth can be enlightening.

Remember Jack Nicholson's famous line "You can't handle the truth!" That is the case sometimes. However, I believe that more often then you realize, people can handle the truth. They certainly don't like it, but they learn to accept it and even flourish from it.

Shaking a snow globe is not for everyone. You have to be ready to accept the good with the bad. You have to be willing to get out of your comfort zone and do things differently. And remember, this is life so there will be more snow storms in your future. You must have the courage to hold on and ride out the unknown instead of running away in search of shelter. It also helps to realize that when the swirling energy comes to rest, your dreams are likely to appear.

It is my wish that I have been able to shake up your snow globe. I hope I have disrupted some of your old ways of thinking

A White Hat & Rose Colored Glasses

and inspired you to embrace the change that is headed your way. Let my words be the snowflakes that will settle back down into something beautiful and exciting. There is something absolutely stunning about the world when it is blanketed in freshly covered pure white snow. May my story of the snow globe, both the shaking and the settling, be the inspiration for a new vision of your future. Finding clarity and taking better actions begins with what else but a white hat and rose colored glasses.

> When you stir up awareness it is the beginning of change

Acknowledgements

I wrote a whole chapter about gratitude so you would think a few paragraphs about appreciation for those who have helped me along the way would be easy, but it is not. I could simply list a whole bunch of names and be done with it but that would not only be boring, it would also be taking the easy way out and that is not a very white hat action to take. Another reason I struggle to write this acknowledgement section is because I truly do try to show appreciation and gratitude at the moment the kindness is given to me. When I say "thank you" I mean it, so what more needs to be said.

Just in case some people didn't hear the thank you the first time around, let me get it down on paper. That way there is no dispute as to how I feel (unless I forget to mention your name and then I'll be in real trouble. But that is an obstacle, not a problem, and I will handle it if the time comes.) So let me start with the crew at Indigo River Publishing. Earl Tillinghast is my editor and many times I have told him that I know he wears a white hat. Earl, thanks for the advice, support, encouragement, and for keeping me right. You are truly one of the good guys. Kyle Weichman is my marketing support and he knows his stuff. He is patient, kind, and has a good business sense. We may not have always agreed on the line between fun and business, but we were always able to work together to get it to come out just fine. And a book doesn't happen on its own so for everyone else at Indigo

A White Hat & Rose Colored Glasses

River who read, proofed, designed, or formatted my words, I thank you all for your effort.

Now if I put on my rose colored glasses, I'm sure I would see thousands of people who inspired, encouraged, motivated or supported me in some small, or large, way. Every kind word, supportive conversation, Like, retweet, or comment all have meaning, yet people can never truly be sure how their actions impacts the world. All I know is that there were many times when something such as a simple word of encouragement was enough to keep me going. Some of my biggest cheerleaders are Ursula Mentjes and Leisa Reid. They saw something in me even before I had the courage to write this second book and start calling myself a writer. You are both awesome at encouraging others to live big and keep those dreams alive.

And now for the family and friends part. It's odd really because we do tend to take our closest friends and family for granted. Too often we forget to be grateful for and appreciate the people that love and support us the most. I hope I don't do that too often but I'm human so I know it happens. Anyway I'd like to acknowledge the old A&S gang. We had good times together and in many ways you were all there with me at the very beginning of my writing career. Every one of you means a lot to me. We have a past that binds us together and I wish nothing but the best for you always.

Vince, Marc, Carol and any and all of you in that circle of friends, I am appreciative of your support in more ways than words can say. For too many years to count, you have played my silly games, listened to my stories, and participated in all of the crazy ideas I wanted to try out for my books. I value the friendship and appreciate your participation. May we all continue to "play" together for many years to come.

When I first thought about my acknowledgments I imagined there would be a paragraph or two and I'd be done, but now it seems like I've hardly even begun. However, I must keep it brief because part of the integrity of my writing is to keep it simple and interesting. Besides to continue on with all of this appreciation stuff might come across a bit too mushy. So let me say thanks to my father because when it comes to thinking differently I know I inherited that gene from you. Plus a huge thank you to my mother for a lifetime of support. You have always believed, encouraged, and loved me. I have no words to express more than that. There are still some other people in my life that should be acknowledged, but maybe I will save that for the next book, plus I'm sure you know who you are so thank you.

And finally, there is Maggie Dea. Earlier I said that we tend to take our closest friends and family for granted and you definitely fall into that category. As hard as I try, I could never express my full appreciation for everything you do. Not to mention the fact that you have probably read and re-read every page and post I have ever written. I think there is a song "Wind beneath my wings" that pretty much describes it all. Thank you doesn't seem enough but it will have to do.

To everyone involved now and in the future let me take a quote from by book:

"Let a heartfelt thank you be enough."

About the Author

Susan Sherbert wrote Grown-Ups Don't Skip and then A White Hat & Rose Colored Glasses because she knows the power of child-like thinking has the potential to change lives.

Her writing career began with a 28-page book about short sheeting a bed that was used by a national linen chain as their free gift with purchase. She has written over 50 original corny joke books and 5 short humor books. She was a humor columnist for several magazines and wrote a Sliver award-winning newsletter of absolutely no importance every month for over twelve years. She is a business owner and an avid golfer. Her big bold dream is to golf every golf course in California.

Susan Sherbert
FunHappyEnjoy.com
714.850.9070
susan@funhappyenjoy.com

The END

(What a good place to start)

www.ingramcontent.com/pod-product-compliance
Lightning Source LLC
Chambersburg PA
CBHW070610300426
44113CB00010B/1481